LINES FOR ALL OCCASIONS

Put-Downs & Zingers

KNOCK KNOCK®

VENICE, CALIFORNIA

Created and published by Knock Knock
Distributed by Who's There Inc.
Venice, CA 90291
knockknockstuff.com

ISBN: 978-160106525-4
UPC: 825703-50115-5

10 9 8 7 6 5

Contents

"Was I drunk when I hired you?"

Introduction

It is a basic human drive to criticize, a need as essential as love and important as freedom. Everyone does it countless times a day—even you. This doesn't make you unkind; even the nicest people habitually practice social or professional critique. We complain to a mate while waiting in an unbearably slow checkout line. We express frustration with reckless drivers, or shout indignation at the TV news. And who hasn't enjoyed a debate on the merits of a given movie, book, or band? Indeed, simple conversation and decision-making are impossible without critical thinking—which is often by necessity insulting to some entity, idea, or person.

Today, with the rise of the Internet and social media, everyone truly is a critic. Online commenting encourages us to spout opinions gratuitously and continuously, creating an environment in which the harshest voices attract the most attention. Like it or not, trading jabs is not only a handy skill, it's also a necessary survival tool.

But what is often lost in this barbed atmosphere is the joy, élan, and pure panache displayed in zingers by great wits of the past.

Anyone can toss off a lazy slur ("You fat pig"), but such digs are a dime a dozen, reflecting poorly on the speaker more than the recipient. What has lasting impact is the one-liner as pithy as it is witty (e.g., "I've had a perfectly wonderful evening. But this wasn't it," as Groucho Marx is said to have quipped while leaving a party thrown by a Beverly Hills socialite). A cutting bon mot justifies its undeniable unpleasantness with a gift of intellect or humor, leaving a trace of dignity in its wake. In fact, it is really a playful opening volley inviting a hearty riposte.

Perhaps no country appreciates witty invective more than Great Britain, a nation with a proud history of acid one-linerism. Public outcry was therefore robust when several Brits were arrested in recent years for the use of supposedly insulting language. Under the Public Order Act 1986, "a person is guilty of an offence if he . . . uses threatening, abusive or insulting words or behaviour." Thanks to this law, and its dubious interpretation by law enforcement officials, an Oxford student was arrested for asking a police officer, "Do you realize your horse is gay?" and a sixteen-year-old was fined for saying "woof" to a dog in front of police officers. In a somewhat more ominous application of the law, a teen was arrested for holding a placard denouncing Scientology, and citizens were arrested for protesting an Islamic political group's stance on homosexuality, women, and Jews.

Actor Rowan Atkinson, aka Mr. Bean, joined the fight against the law, challenging its "chilling effect on free expression and free protest." Thanks to him and others, the House of Lords voted in late 2012 to remove the word "insulting" from the law.

Clearly, then, the ability to taunt others is not merely a privilege to be enjoyed, but a liberty to be utilized lest it be lost. It is this book's intention to help you exercise that right with regularity and confidence. Moreover, the book will help you toss quips with zestful enjoyment and, best of all, style. In this way, you will help to make the world a safer place not only for free speech, but also for wit and good taste.

APPEARANCE

When you can judge a book by its cover

MANY OTHERWISE INTELLIGENT people suffer from the notion that mocking someone's physicality makes one appear childish, base, or—far worse—stupid. Such individuals censor their natural drive to critique and attack, resulting in a false politeness that does no good and merely stifles open and honest communication.

The Truth Hurts

We know Americans are fat. Since 1990, men's average weight has crept from 180 to 196 pounds, and women's from 142 to 156, according to a 2012 Gallup poll. But fat-denial has also increased: men considered 171 pounds their "ideal" weight in 1990; today it's 185. Women considered 129 pounds ideal in 1990; today they'd be happy at 140. Clearly, America desperately needs a wakeup call. Armed with this book, you're just the patriot to provide it.

As we must admit in moments of honesty, such artifice flies in the very face of human instinct. We need look no further than our own children for proof. Unspoiled by adult hypocrisy, the very young understand the power of attacking others' superficial flaws—and apply this knowledge on schoolyards around the world every day. Let us strive to be childlike: honest, free, and artless in our responses to the world. In the cosmic scheme, fraudulent "maturity" is far more contemptible than the sincere expression of scorn against those who have it coming.

And who's to say that skin-deep failures really are skin-deep? Slovenly dress, lackluster hygiene, and unappealing presentation often express a deeper flaw than any physical imperfection. To show up for work, and life, looking unat-tractive or unkempt is in itself an insulting sign of disregard for others, for the world, and even for oneself. Indeed, if more of us had the courage to slander each other's appearance, the world would be, on balance, a more considerate, civi-lized, and well-groomed place.

Ugly

Are you what the cat dragged in?

That really is a face only a
mother could love.

When you were born, the
doctor screamed.

If that's not a mask, you
should totally get one.

You know what you'd look great
in? A full-body burlap sack.

You're so ugly it hurts my feelings.

Do you still love nature, despite
what it did to you?

Whoever gave you a 10 should
get back some change.

———•·•———

Are you recycling those
bags under your eyes?

———•·•———

Did it hurt when you fell from
heaven? Because it looks like
you landed on your face.

———•·•———

Your picture is worth a
thousand words, and all of
them are synonyms for ugly.

———•·•———

Your baby is beautiful. Is she yours?

———•·•———

Oh my God, look at you. Was
anyone else hurt in the accident?

———•·•———

Is that your face, or are you
breaking it in for a bulldog?

Fat

I've heard of XL, and XXL, but
MCMXL is a new one.

Where'd you find a cow large
enough to make that belt?

You must have your own ZIP code.

I guess you're on the seefood diet:
you see food and then you eat it.

Supersize Me was an exposé, not a how-to.

Your body is, in fact, too
bootylicious for me.

Inside every fat person is a skinny person
trying to get out. In your case, two.

It's good to see you. Just
not that much of you.

Your feet called. They miss seeing you.

You could stand to lose a few
pounds. On second thought,
maybe you'd better sit.

Are you collecting chins?

These Walls Can Talk

One-liners are an ancient art, as proven by
graffiti discovered in Pompeii—a city frozen
in ash from Mt. Vesuvius in AD 79. A few pithy
Pompeiian epithets include: "Phileros is a
eunuch," "Oh Chius, I hope that your ulcerous
pustules reopen and burn even more than they
did before," and "O wall, I am amazed that you
have not fallen down since you support the
loathsome scribblings of so many writers."

Skinny

Was that "feed the world"
song about you?

———•—•———

Do you count using your
fingers, toes, and ribs?

———•—•———

If you had a food blog it
would be a blank page.

———•—•———

You're so skinny even your
patience is wearing thin.

———•—•———

Do you bathe with an inner tube?

———•—•———

You put the die in diet.

———•—•———

You're so thin, you
swallowed a meatball and
thought you were pregnant.

You have to run around in
the shower to get wet.

———•◦•———

You'd be a great model for a
stick-figure drawing class.

Poor Hygiene

Something smells fishy—I'm
guessing it's you.

———•◦•———

It wouldn't kill you to use deodorant,
but it might kill me if you don't.

———•◦•———

They make yellowing toothpaste?

———•◦•———

Did something die in your mouth?

———•◦•———

Sasquatch lives!

———•◦•———

I didn't know teeth could grow fur.

Give As Good As You Get

If you receive a looks-based insult, no matter how well deserved, preserve your dignity with a quality retort from the "Dunderheads" section in the next chapter, or try a classic comeback: "Oh look, it can talk." • "Do you feel better about yourself now?" • "You say that like it's a bad thing." • "Your boyfriend/girlfriend doesn't seem to mind." • "I bet you were up all night trying to come up with that one." • "Did I give you permission to talk?"

What crawled up your shirt and croaked?

You smell so bad, you draw more flies than an entomological artist.

Please breathe the other way. You're bleaching my hair.

Did your dog mark you?

Old Age

Tell me more about the Paleolithic Era.

—•—

Stupid Old Joke called. They want their lame back.

—•—

Wrinkles tell stories, or, in your case, epic novels.

—•—

Even the oldies station sounds like noise to you.

—•—

Did you honeymoon in Pompeii?

—•—

You remember a time before cell phones—and, for that matter, Morse code.

—•—

You've had your face lifted so many times I'm surprised there's anything left in your shoes.

You're so old Jesus owes you money.

Many things improve with
age. You are not one of them.

Was your birth announcement
printed on papyrus?

I see you've got skintight jeans to
go with your skintight face.

Shouldn't you be at a
bingo tournament?

Callow Youth

You don't know what we did
before the Internet, do you?

You're so young, you just stopped
wearing Velcro shoes.

You still think the world needs you.

You're so young, you think "hey, baby" is just a statement of fact.

If you drank from the fountain of youth, you'd be a fetus.

You're so young, you think a senior discount is for twelfth graders.

I'd invite you to dinner but it's past your bedtime.

Life is short, and so is your list of accomplishments.

I'd slap you but I don't want to be arrested for child abuse.

Poor Style

Are you in costume?

That's a one-of-a-kind piece—and
there's a reason no one else wanted it.

You're wearing that ironically, right?

The fashion police have a citation for you.

Money can't buy taste, can it?

I didn't know the childless
could wear mom jeans.

Sorry, I couldn't hear you
over your outfit.

Nice outfit. Is your burlap
sack at the cleaners?

Was there a sale at Goodwill?

———•◦•———

If you're in the Hair Club for Men, cancel your membership.

———•◦•———

Who does your hair? I want to make sure I don't go to her.

———•◦•———

I didn't know the painted whore look was in.

Tip: Tactical Humility

To charm friends and preemptively disarm bullies, jab yourself. "By self-deprecating a little, you're making sure [others] aren't expecting too much and you gain points for modesty," says Mark Leary, professor of psychology and neuroscience at Duke University. Emulate Phyllis Diller, queen of auto-insults such as "A peeping Tom threw up on my windowsill" and "My body's in such bad shape I wear prescription underwear."

PERSONALITY

When deep down they're jerks

THOSE UNFORTUNATE SOULS
afflicted with social or personality
impairments are aware, if only on a
subconscious level, that something
is very wrong with them. Unfortunately, the same flaws that turn
them into irritating social pariahs
also prevent them from honest
self-examination and improvement. In such cases, a well-timed
put-down of the offending party's

Multicultural Malignance

Slandering someone's brains or personality isn't always the most effective mode of insult, especially abroad. In Italy and Latin America, the surest means of offense is trashing a person's mother, while Dutch natives often mention disease or disability in their slams. In Arab regions, exposing the sole of your shoe is as offensive as it gets, while in East Asia, touching or patting someone on the head does the trick.

psyche, manner, or habits can serve a double function. It may not only provide catharsis to the giver, but also the blessing of enlightenment, however painful, to the recipient.

Therefore we must never shrink from tossing barbs of a personal nature at the neurotic and personality-challenged among us. Indeed, for some, such a zinger may provide relief from the agony of mental isolation: to be accurately disparaged is to be recognized and understood, a rare gift in life. Throwing such a jab also implies that the insultee is worth the effort, which may in itself provide some hope to the socially hopeless. Finally, by illuminating an annoying person's flaws, a skilled heckler makes it possible for the un-self-aware to begin the process of improvement. As a bonus, the daring social critic also provides a service to each person the offending individual meets in future: when next someone tells him, "You're crazy," he won't be able to say he's never heard it before.

Nuts & Crazies

I don't have enough sandbags to hold
off the storm surge of your crazy.

———◆———

Every one of your multiple
personalities thinks you're nuts.

———◆———

You made a left turn at eccentric and
are heading straight toward batshit.

———◆———

Too bad you're not the
entertaining kind of insane.

———◆———

When you chose your path,
was it labeled socio?

———◆———

You're not crazy like a fox—you're
crazy like a crazy person.

———◆———

Paranoid? I'll say. Everybody's
always getting together to talk
about how paranoid you are.

Your sanity left no forwarding address.

If you were a number, you'd be irrational.

Is it hard being the mayor of Crazytown?

Cheats & Liars

I met more interesting liars
in kindergarten.

Did you model your integrity
after a tobacco executive?

You're in a dysfunctional
relationship with the truth.

You need to get yourself
some fireproof pants.

Your ass must be jealous of all the
crap that comes out of your mouth.

When it comes to sincerity,
you're full of it.

I didn't know snakes could
lie through their teeth.

Do you wash both faces in the morning?

You inherited some good values, but
through diligent hard work, you
managed to overcome them.

Dunderheads

I'd insult you back, but I
don't think you'd get it.

Did you have to repeat preschool?

You spent twenty minutes
looking at an orange juice box
because it said "concentrate."

You could never get smart
with me, could you?

———•◆•———

I don't want to blow your mind,
but LMNOP is not a letter.

———•◆•———

It takes you two hours to
watch *60 Minutes*.

———•◆•———

Did someone pee in your gene pool?

The Gore-y Details

Literary titan Gore Vidal relished attacking
other writers, calling Truman Capote's death a
"good career move" and declaring "The three
saddest words in the English language are
'Joyce Carol Oates.'" He compared Norman
Mailer to Charles Manson and William F.
Buckley Jr. to Hitler, and called John Updike
"another boring little middle-class boy hus-
tling his way to the top." That puts the *ouch*
in *touché*.

I'm dumbfounded by what you just said. I found it really dumb.

Thanks for giving me a piece of your mind. I know you don't have much to spare.

If I stand close enough to you, I can hear the ocean.

If you had an "I'm With Stupid" shirt, the arrow would just point up.

You're as sharp as a very dull knife.

Did you already spend all your common sense?

Great minds think alike, which explains why we have nothing in common.

There's only one thing smaller than
your intellect, and I'm sure you
don't want to talk about that.

I'd jump into this conversation,
but I'm afraid I'd hit my
head on the bottom.

When your IQ reaches
60, you should sell.

Negative Nellies

It's not everyone who can find
the bad in every situation.

Your first-world problems must
have your friends crying in their
hand-poured artisanal coffees.

You're a glass-totally-empty
kind of a person, aren't you?

Tip: Don't Troll for Trouble

Beware: truly anonymous online commenting is a thing of the past. In a 2012 Texas lawsuit, a day spa owner and a prominent attorney sued anonymous commenters over posts claiming the couple were sexual deviants, molesters, and drug dealers. The haters were unmasked and initially slammed with almost $14 million in damages. Though the case continued to be litigated, the lesson remains: you can hide your name, but not your IP address.

Do you complain in your sleep?

————◆————

I guess if you expect nothing,
you'll never be disappointed.

————◆————

When life gives you lemons,
do you make funeral arrangements?

————◆————

Any more whine out of you and
we could start a vineyard.

Pollyannas

Your ass must burn from all the
sunshine coming out of it.

—•—

Your enthusiasm is
infectious—like a disease.

—•—

Have you considered developing
an addiction to downers?

—•—

You're about as genuine as a $3 bill.

—•—

I understand you're happy, but
should we all have to suffer for it?

—•—

A bad mood would be a
refreshing change for you.

—•—

Your cup runneth over with
oh my god shut up.

Bores

Enough about you—let's talk
about something interesting.

You're about as scintillating
as a dial tone.

Are you still talking? I fell asleep.

I've seen wallpaper with
more personality.

Spending alone time with you makes
me wish I spent more time alone.

You should market yourself
as a cure for insomnia.

I'm so glad I have this smartphone
to amuse me while you speak.

I admire your confidence in
assuming I give a shit.

You're so boring, I heard you
put your dog to sleep.

We all have issues; I just
don't care about yours.

There's someone out there
for everyone—have you tried
writing to inmates?

Is this a bedtime story or are
you just incredibly boring?

Please, go on. I always yawn
when I'm interested.

I know you're trying . . .
very trying.

Losers

You're not so much a has-
been as a never-will-be.

———•———

Someone has to be below average.

———•———

Do you have any achievements
in real life?

———•———

The difference between
champ and chump is "u."

———•———

It's not everyone who can be
satisfied with mediocrity.

———•———

How often do you leave your
parents' basement?

———•———

I'm sick of you and your
delusions of adequacy.

Everyone's good at something.
You're good at sucking at stuff.

———

Should I send a search party
for your hidden talent?

———

When I think of all the people
I respect the most, you're right
there, serving them drinks.

Every Dog Has Its Day

Each generation needs a Don Rickles, and
Triumph the Insult Comic Dog is the zinger-
meister for the early 21st century. With his
Eastern-European-accented jibes and disdain
for political correctness, comedian Robert
Smigel's cigar-smoking puppet skewers
everyone from Bon Jovi to to Occupy Wall St.
protesters. His highest praise, reserved for
few (including Rickles), is a request to "sniff
your butt."

Assholes, Egomaniacs, & Narcissists

I think you're great, but I'm a
notoriously lousy judge of character.

———•———

You must have great upper body
strength from climbing over all
those people on your way up.

———•———

At least you're not phony. You want
to be hated for who you really are.

———•———

Did they name jerk chicken after you?

———•———

I wish I were as beautiful
as you think you are.

———•———

How often did your parents
tell you that you're special?

———•———

How do you fit all that ego in
an average-sized body?

I'd like you to have more self-esteem, but you don't deserve it.

———•—•———

You're so cheap you can't even pay attention.

———•—•———

Let's play horse. I'll be the front end and you be yourself.

———•—•———

I believe the best career path for you would be selling your own organs on the black market.

———•—•———

The next time you shave, could you stand a little closer to the razor?

———•—•———

I'm looking forward to the pleasure of your company— since I haven't had it yet.

———•—•———

Even Mr. Rogers thinks you're an ass.

"LIFESTYLES"

When people become clichés

ONE OF THE MORE IRKSOME
aspects of life in the 21st century
is the epidemic of "hipness" among
dimwitted, herd-following urban
denizens. Lacking the necessary
critical faculties to generate an
original worldview or personal
style, the subcultural phony relies
heavily upon his homogeneous peer
group for cues on behavior, dress,
political views, social norms, and
leisure activities.

Thanks for the Meme-ories

Internet memes—viral photos, videos, or phrases, often digitally tweaked for laughs—are a new way to put down entire social groups and events. In 2012, a shot of gymnast McKayla Maroney's "not impressed" face was swiftly coopted to indicate disapproval of hipsters, the royal wedding, and Mark Zuckerberg. Even President Obama mimicked Maroney's expression when the two met in the Oval Office, cementing its status.

In contrast to the self-appointed "cool kids" of previous generations, however, contemporary hip types are distinctly self-conscious wimps, unable to embrace enthusiasm without many layers of protective irony. Conveniently, this also makes them ideal targets for your incisive wit. One might even argue that today's hipster/foodie/eco-freak not only invites satire but subconsciously seeks it, since he is admittedly miserable, lost in a digitally addicted, bike-riding, gourmet food-trucking facsimile of real life. When you dare to point out that the poseur has no clothes, you not only do him a favor, but you also strike a larger blow for the embattled cultural forces of common sense and true style, whose hegemony has been on the wane for decades.

Unfortunately, hipsters are only part of the problem. Other lifestyle offenders include the chemically addled (who spread drama), and intellectual, political, or religious snobs (who spread judgment). Like the hipster, these wet blankets can cast a certain pall on the proceedings, but they mustn't be allowed to. It's up to you, the sensible independent thinker—and skilled faultfinder—to put them in their place.

Hipsters

I bet you don't even need those glasses.

I know you think you're
unique, but you look like
everyone else in this dive bar.

I'm sorry your favorite band
has a popular song.

If I heard this band on vinyl,
would they suck any less?

It must take forever to look like
you just rolled out of bed.

I wish you were as cool as
you think you are.

I bet that tattoo is going to
look great in fifty years.

Are you sponsored by
Pabst Blue Ribbon?

———•◆•———

You're such a hipster, your
beard wears glasses.

———•◆•———

Careful with that porkpie hat—
after forty, you're at greater risk
of breaking your hipster.

———•◆•———

What did it cost to get
your goatee imported
from Brooklyn?

———•◆•———

It looks like your
Foreigner T-shirt is
wearing *you* ironically.

———•◆•———

What do you weigh? An instagram?

———•◆•———

Hipster.

Pseudo-Intellectuals

Doesn't your neck get tired
holding up that gigantic brain?

Oh yeah, I read some
philosophy in college, too.

Sartre was talking about you when
he said, "Hell is other people."

You can keep talking, but I
won't keep listening.

I'm no expert, but neither are you.

You must have had a lot of pseudo-
education to become such an
accomplished pseudo-intellectual.

I think I may have just sprained
my eyeballs from rolling them.

New-Agers, Vegans, & Eco-Freaks

The only reason you care about animals
so much is that people hate you.

❖

Nice altar. You do know
we're not in India.

❖

You're awfully judgmental of people
who aren't as open-minded as you.

Vilifying the Hubristic

A truly pleonastic insulter will baffle and
perplex pompous pseudo-intellectuals by using
multisyllabic and arcane words to describe the
cognoscitive inadequacies of others. Using as
insults words like nescient, benighted, fatu-
itous, insensate, gormless, Boeotian, puerile,
or oscitant has the double benefit of not only
conveying their appropriate meaning, but also
fortuitiously making the insultee even more
abashed by his ignorance of the term itself.

I fake-like this fake chicken.

What's your spirit animal—jackass?

I'd like to see those yoga
pants in corpse pose.

How can you meditate over the
sound of your own smugness?

I think it's great that you
recycle your clothes.

Your food may be sustainable
but your attitude sure isn't.

I'm not global warming up to
your eco-friendly personality.

I'm going to put a carbon
footprint on your face.

Food Snobs

Wow, you can really taste the
pretension in this microfoam.

Taking photos of your lunch does
not make you a food critic.

This tastes like organic, locally
grown, humanely farmed crap.

I'd like to cleanse my palate
and never eat this again.

Just because you can pickle, cure, or
smoke it doesn't mean you should.

This fried seitan looks like
dog food. Is that the idea?

Please stop calling your crawl
space the cheese cave.

Tip: #HashItOut

As modes of trash-talk change, one new angle is employing hashtags—a # sign followed by a brief descriptor. Originally intended as search tools on social media, hashtags are now also used as demeaning postscripts or snarky asides to otherwise mild posts (#epicfail, for example). But before using a hashtag, check its readability. For example, singer Susan Boyle's PR team is regretting #susanalbumparty.

Druggies & Drunks

Please have a drink—you're a mean sober.

———

That much weed and you're still uptight?

———

Are you this stupid when you're sober?

———

Actually, you're not a fun drunk.

You've confused *Fear and Loathing in Las Vegas* with an instruction manual.

————

Bouncers have a special headlock named after you.

————

When you drink, you have to go to court to find out what happened.

————

Friends accuse you of "acting weird" whenever they meet you sober.

————

Your AA sponsor is Absolut.

————

Is there anything you haven't tried to turn into a bong?

————

A six-pack doesn't qualify as a support group.

Did you forget to steal someone
else's medication today?

———

If I wanted someone to puke and
fall on me, I would have had kids.

Ideologues

Don't let the facts get in the
way of your opinions.

———

Jesus wept because he knew
you'd be one of his followers.

———

Does it get terribly stuffy in that
cloak of self-righteousness?

———

If I put coal up your butt, could
you make me a diamond?

———

If ignorance is bliss, you should be the
happiest person alive.

The Mormons called. They
think you're a little uptight.

———·•·———

Instead of being born again, why
don't you just grow up?

———·•·———

You're so tight your ass squeaks.

Slackers & Layabouts

If the secret to success is
showing up, you're doomed.

———·•·———

You make sloths look ambitious.

———·•·———

An A for effort would be
insulting to effort.

———·•·———

It's nice to know I can always
count on you to flake.

You spend more time on the
couch than a therapist's dog.

Glaciers drag themselves across
the tundra faster than you.

You're flakier than my
grandmother's pie crust.

I've seen pantyhose run
faster than you.

You're so lazy you can't
even breathe hard.

I don't know where I'd be without
you, but you'd be totally screwed.

Pretty sure you're not
supposed to use adult diapers
in lieu of the loo.

Dog Park Divas

Is your dog in heat, or just slutty?

———•—•———

What kind of dog is that?
Cockapoo-shit?

———•—•———

After a while, dog owners really
do start to resemble their dogs.

Foodie Fight

New York Times critic Pete Wells wrote a brutal
2012 review of chef Guy Fieri's Times Square
eatery ("When we hear the words Donkey
Sauce, which part of the donkey are we
supposed to think about?"). Fieri fans called
Wells elitist while foodies lauded his candor.
No harm done, though: in light of the review,
ironic New Yorkers flocked to the restaurant
out of sheer curiosity. Sounds like a win-win.

Since when do they allow
rats in the dog park?

———•·•———

Is that leash for you or the dog?

———•·•———

I see dog whispering isn't working.
Have you tried shouting?

Gym Jerks

There's a reason they
give you towels here.

———•·•———

Can you bench-press your ego?

———•·•———

Those stairs go nowhere.
You know that, right?

———•·•———

For someone who spends
all her free time at the gym,
you sure don't look it.

Sorry, I'm not fluent in grunt.

Easy on the makeup. It's a
gym, not clown college.

Passive-Aggressive Types

I always forget the exact
definition of passive-aggressive.
Thanks for the reminder.

You don't need to be passive-aggressive
to get a rise out of me; your normal
personality does that just fine.

So, was your mom passive and your dad
aggressive or was it the other way around?

Why don't you try passive-
passive for a change of pace?

Your passive-aggressive tendencies go
so well with your victim complex.

NEAR & DEAR

When they're too close for comfort

HOPEFULLY YOU'RE BEGINNING to learn from this volume how important it is to maintain a healthy arsenal of witty, incisive zingers with which to defend yourself and promote the larger goal of a sane, civilized world. It's never too late—nor too early— to start learning how to effectively deliver slights and slurs. If insults are a form of kindness, as

Not a Good Thing

Sometimes the best comeback is no comeback. When Martha Stewart impugned her "friend" Rachael Ray's cooking in a 2009 interview, Ray took the high road, admitting that Stewart's skills were "far beyond" hers. In the end, Ray came out on top: after Stewart's show was cancelled, Ray moved into Martha's old studio. Revenge is indeed a dish best served cold—whatever one's culinary ability.

they clearly can be, then charity most certainly begins at home.

The family unit provides our first experience of society, a microcosm of the larger world, where we first are taught acceptable—and unacceptable—behaviors. This makes the home the ideal environment in which to learn not only how to act, but also how to censure those who do not meet our needs, expectations, and desires. From earliest childhood we should begin to practice critical volleys at the dinner table, in the car, and elsewhere. The bonus of grasping how to lampoon others from a young age is that it prepares one for the cruelty and insensitivity of the "real" world—and of other children. As discussed, schoolyards can be battlefields, and every child deserves to enter it well armed.

Furthermore, one must admit that our nearest loved ones deserve our best efforts at brutal, therapeutic honesty. Should we reserve our most constructive criticisms for friends and strangers? Of course not. Why would we expect any less of our relatives and friends than we do of the DMV lady?

Between Parents & Children

Your parenting has guaranteed
years of income for my therapist.

Coming home to visit makes me
stronger—because it doesn't kill me.

I'm sorry I inherited
your worst traits.

You'd go to the ends of the earth for
us, Mom. But would you stay there?

Dinner was excellent.
Just ask the dog.

You could be a great comfort in my
old age, if you weren't causing it.

I'd prefer a helicopter parent
to a dive-bomber parent.

Turns out, giving birth to
you was the easy part.

———•—•———

It's not just you; I call all of my
children Satan's minions.

Siblings

Mom sold you to the gypsies,
but they sent you back.

———•—•———

I wanted to get a pet lizard, but
Mom and Dad got you instead.

———•—•———

You were an accident—Mom tripped
and fell on the next-door neighbor.

———•—•———

Someone had to inherit the
crazy gene in our family.

———•—•———

Good thing Mom figured out
parenting by the time she got to me.

You're the sap in our family tree.

Mom liked you best, but Dad
thought you were a putz.

I wish you were more like
the brother I never had.

Extended Family

Spending time with you
helps me understand why my
mom is so screwed up.

You're my favorite creepy uncle.

I look forward to your
oversharing every Christmas.

From the looks of it, your
cousins did more than kiss.

We're not losing a son; we're gaining a controlling shrew.

———

We wanted our daughter to marry a kind, intelligent person, but one out of two isn't bad.

———

This family has more nuts than a squirrel with hoarding issues.

Take That, Tiger Mom

Before condemning your folks, consider China's Xiao Baiyou, aka "Wolf Dad," who says he beat his kids between ages three and twelve, when "kids are mainly animals." "I have more than a thousand rules . . . If you don't follow the rules, then I must beat you." As his eldest observes, "Though Dad likes using traditional educational methods . . . there may be some distance from the best results."

Ever since I saw you in our family
tree I've wanted to cut it down.

We don't complain about
your shortcomings but about
your long stayings.

The difference between in-laws and
outlaws is that outlaws are wanted.

Bad Friends

You're my best frenemy.

I love when you cancel plans
at the last minute—it gives me
more time to find new friends.

I like friends like you who are uglier
than I am. It boosts my self-esteem.

I'll never forget the first time
we met, but I'll keep trying.

Leaving so soon? I was about
to poison your drink.

———•—•———

I didn't enjoy running into
you, but my car did.

———•—•———

If a friend is someone you
know very well and like anyway,
what should I call you?

———•—•———

It's not me, it's you.

———•—•———

It's important to me to have friends
I can rely on—that's why I have
other friends besides you.

———•—•———

Of all the people I've met you're
certainly one of them.

———•—•———

You're unforgettable. I keep
trying to forget you exist.

Offensive Offenses

In 1977 former college professor Reinhold Aman founded *Maledicta: The International Journal of Verbal Aggression*, a semi-scholarly periodical dedicated to the study of offensive, insulting, scatological, and obscene language. Sadly, in 1993 Aman was sentenced to eighteen months in prison for sending his ex-wife threatening, hate-filled postcards. As Nietzsche said, "If you gaze for long into an abyss, the abyss gazes also into you."

Lovers

I think the blindfold is a great idea if we're going to have sex.

No, it's not your weird fetish; it's you.

I don't think we can be "friends with benefits" when there's no benefit.

Are you sure this
isn't your first time?

———•·•———

I'd rather pass a kidney stone
than another night with you.

———•·•———

There was something about you
that I liked, but you spent it.

———•·•———

You're not a bad lover,
just . . . different.

———•·•———

I'd rather spoon with a
praying mantis.

———•·•———

It's called foreplay, not one play.

———•·•———

I'd give you a map if I thought it
could help you find my G-spot.

———•·•———

Don't mistake my groans of
pain for moans of pleasure.

Lotharios & Leches

Do you have a punch card
at the free clinic?

———•◦•———

I'm not your type. I'm not inflatable.

———•◦•———

I totally want you—to go away.

———•◦•———

You are validating my inherent
mistrust of strangers.

———•◦•———

I'm not that desperate and
you're not that lucky.

———•◦•———

With men like you in the world,
vibrator sales must be going up.

———•◦•———

When you date a woman,
do you arrive at the door with
flowers and antibiotics?

You'd think by now you'd have
found everyone willing to
sleep with you.

———•∘•———

Have you considered a career
in sanitation? You're great
at picking up trash.

———•∘•———

You can buy me a drink but
I'd like to enjoy it alone.

———•∘•———

I hope you are sterile.

———•∘•———

Sorry, I already have one ass in
my pants; I don't need two.

———•∘•———

Does your "masturbator's elbow"
make it difficult to lift that beer?

———•∘•———

I like your approach. Let's
see your departure.

Sluts & Romantic Rivals

You've never met a man you didn't like—for at least fifteen minutes.

You're bisexual? How often do you buy sex?

What's your favorite position—yes, absolutely?

It may be time to rediscover your inhibitions.

I'm against slut-shaming but I'll make an exception in your case.

The dress code is business casual. Do you work in a whorehouse?

I keep extra lovers around since I figure you'll steal at least one.

My first thought about you was that
you were slutty and a terrible dresser.
I was wrong. You are a fine dresser.

———————

You've got a body that won't quit
and a brain that won't start.

———————

I've heard you know how to say "Where
are my pants?" in seven languages.

Tip: Good Luck Is Bad Luck

It's always wise to insult a friend before a
theatrical performance—in fact, artists around
the world consider "good luck" to be akin to a
curse. For actors, "break a leg" is the appropriate pre-curtain sentiment, while dancers appre-
ciate a hearty *merde* (French for excrement).
Opera singers should be wished *toi toi toi* (an
onomatopoetic phrase imitating the sound of
spitting). And if your friend speaks Spanish, go
with *mucha mierda* (lots of excrement).

OTHER PEOPLE

When you venture out in public

IN NO SITUATION IS IT MORE crucial to have one's quiver packed with handy taunts than when dealing with the riffraff of the rat race: coworkers, baristas, meter maids, telemarketers, and other public enemies. The reason is as silly as it is unfortunate: simply because formal introductions have not been made, many people subconsciously believe interactions with strangers

Tip: Don't Let Them Win

Posting online rants about companies' deplorable customer service or defective products can provide consumer catharsis, as well as a valuable warning to others. Unfortunately, it may also push the offending vendor's name higher in Internet search results. Google is aware of this phenomenon and has made efforts to revise its algorithms, but, for now, it appears that there really is no such thing as bad publicity—especially on the Internet.

don't count. They feel as if no one is watching, and therefore their actions have no consequences.

As these people's intellectual superior, you have a social duty to make such people know you, and understand that someone is, indeed, keeping tabs on their behavior: you. It doesn't matter if they are above or below you in social rank, wealth, or age. Rude is rude, drunk is drunk, incompetent is incompetent.

Sadly, no one ever became a nicer coworker or more courteous customer-service agent without being threatened in some way. Such a threat from a stranger may serve as a reality check, a warning to shape up while there's still time. But even if your words have no immediate positive impact on the culprit's behavior, you will still be justified in offering searing indictments of others' lousy service or behavior: you are a victim, a canary in the coal mine of their incompetence. Fight back. Who knows? Someday they may thank you for saving them from the axe—and from themselves.

Bureaucrats and Public Authorities

Did you go to remedial
DMV-employee school?

I'd call you a pompous ass but
I don't want to insult donkeys.

Did the city hire you because they
don't have to pay benefits to zombies?

Your attention to the details of
this job would impress Kafka.

I thought "faceless bureaucrat"
was just a saying.

Do you need training to be a court
officer or just a shiny badge?

Which circle of hell do you preside
over in your spare time?

Customer Service Hacks

If you ever leave your job in tech support you could easily find work as a condescending turd.

What crimes did you commit in your previous life to become a telemarketer in this one?

You've made great use of your fifteen minutes of customer service training.

May I speak to your manager? I want to see if he is also laughably incompetent.

Do you practice your rude delivery or is it natural?

I got more useful customer service from your hold music.

You're like a used-car salesman
without the charm.

⸻

What number do I press
to talk to a machine?

Drivers, Parkers, & Meter Maids

What would Jesus do?
Unlike you, Jesus would
use his turn signal.

⸻

When do you get your license?

⸻

Unless that's the Batmobile, you
only need one parking space.

⸻

Are you colorblind or just
unaware that green means go?

⸻

Did you get your license from
a Cracker Jack box?

If you drove any slower
we'd be in a parade.

———•—•———

Obviously you don't think and drive.

———•—•———

When you were little, did you
ticket Matchbox cars?

———•—•———

It's hard to take a person who
drives a golf cart seriously.

Name-Calling—Literally

Like Waterloo and Watergate, political barbs
are often eponymous. *Quisling* (traitor)
was coined for Norwegian Nazi ally Vidkun
Quisling, while *gerrymander* (to draw unfair,
often oddly shaped voting districts) blends
Massachusetts governor Elbridge Gerry with
salamander. *Willie Hortonize*—to exploit racial
bias in campaigns—refers to a sensationalistic
TV ad that helped sink Michael Dukakis' White
House bid.

People Who Wait On Us

I'll take a grande latte without
the grande attitude.

If I promise not to complain
about the service, do you promise
not to spit on my food?

I'll take the #23—same as your IQ.

Here's a big tip: get another job.

I'm sorry if my shopping
has interfered with
your lousy work ethic.

I'd take my business elsewhere,
but I'm a masochist.

I didn't order extra ego
with this pizza.

Coworkers

A professional wardrobe
shouldn't be based on
the oldest profession.

———•—•———

Failure is indeed an
option when I have
to work with you.

———•—•———

Casual Friday refers to
clothing, not hygiene.

———•—•———

There is no "I" in team;
there is also no "SOB."

———•—•———

Thanks! Your crappy work
makes me look great.

———•—•———

Do you save up all your
lazy for the office?

Hometown Harassment

People often associate their personal identity with the area in which they were born and raised. So consider flinging the regional insult, which can run from the macro to the micro: "America is a large, friendly dog in a very small room. Every time it wags its tail, it knocks over a chair." —Arnold Toynbee • "California is a nice place to live—if you happen to be an orange." —Fred Allen • "I love New York City. I've got a gun." —Charles Barkley

Do you have a black belt
in brownnosing?

Your brain is perpetually
Out of Office.

Someone with your
qualifications should go
far—and never come back.

Overlings & Underlings

Do you deliberately base
your management style on
the Spanish Inquisition?

———•◦•———

It takes a true micro-intelligence to
be so good at micro-managing.

———•◦•———

Was I drunk when I hired you?

———•◦•———

Saying you have a lousy work ethic
implies you have a work ethic.

———•◦•———

You didn't get my email?
I sent it to horribleboss@
worstjobever.com.

———•◦•———

You put the ass in assistant.

———•◦•———

Apparently there *are*
stupid questions.

Neighbors

You were so loud last night, I
feel like we had a threesome.

What's your landscaping
strategy? Au naturel?

Are those cars on cinder
blocks art pieces?

We've canceled cable. Listening to your
fights is our preferred entertainment.

How are those tap lessons coming along?

I guess you don't need a security system
since your dog barks all the time.

Whoever said the grass is always
greener never lived next to you.

Lousy Parents

I can't wait to hear
what your kid says
about you in therapy.

———•••———

Are you going to leash him?

———•••———

All babies are different—
yours is *really* different.

———•••———

Cute kid. Is she feral?

———•••———

Maybe one day he'll run
away from home.

———•••———

Do you pay the cable company
extra to watch your kids?

———•••———

Have you considered installing
a GPS device on your kids?

When did you get your
helicopter license?

Your children are so well traveled.
They walk all over you.

Citizens with Poor Manners

We'd all enjoy your phone
conversation if your life were
remotely interesting.

You can't cut in line—
there's no room for your giant
sense of entitlement.

Keep it down—
everyone can hear
what an idiot you are.

Were you born with a silver
spoon up your butt?

Could you talk a little louder? I
don't think God heard you.

Just because you were born
in a barn doesn't mean you
have to eat like a pig.

Those wolves that raised
you must be so proud.

A New (Old) Low

Every campaign season brings cries against
vicious attack ads, but such tactics are
nothing new. Thomas Paine called George
Washington "the patron of the fraud," and
papers labeled Abraham Lincoln "a fourth-
rate lecturer." John Quincy Adams said
Congressman John Randolph's "tongue drips
poison"; Randolph in turn said Secretary of
State Edward Livingston "shines and stinks
like rotten mackerel by moonlight."

FAMOUS FACE-OFFS

When notables aren't very nice

MOST CELEBRITIES STRIVE IN
public to appear secure, confi-
dent, and evolved to the point of
near-perfection. What the hoi
polloi don't realize is that, in fact,
celebrities become famous precisely
because they are more insecure
than the rest of us, and are willing
to sacrifice much more in pursuit
of attention. For some, this desperation is not tempered by the

Turn Up the Heat

Originating at New York's Friar's Club in 1949, celebrity roasts provided comedians and actors the means to privately, wickedly mock one another, a tradition the general public was allowed to enjoy when *The Dean Martin Celebrity Roast* began airing in 1974. Now, Comedy Central hosts its own brand of B-level-celebrity ridicule-fests, which are often more mean-spirited and filthy than anything Dino was ever allowed to broadcast.

achievement of success, and may even be intensified within the crucible of celebrity, much like pottery fired in a kiln. For once you have achieved fame, wealth, power, and adulation, your work to hang onto them has only begun.

This is truer now in the era of the twenty-four-hour news cycle, but celebrities have always taunted, teased, and backstabbed one another. Sometimes it's in the name of friendly sport; sometimes it's mutually beneficial. The history of the arts is filled with examples of fruitful rivalry among giants, from Shakespeare and Christopher Marlowe to Tupac and Biggie. Indeed, true greatness is not achievable without creative competition.

Fans also benefit from battles between idols, and the uglier the better. When titans toss mud in each other's eyes they provide both great entertainment and an emotionally reassuring reminder that "having it all" is no guarantee of contentment, wisdom, or even good taste.

Celebs on Talent

"I deny I ever said that actors are cattle. What I said was, 'Actors should be *treated* like cattle.'" —Alfred Hitchcock

---

"I would trust her totally on cottage cheese." —Restaurant critic Gael Greene, on restaurant critic Mimi Sheraton

---

"Bill Clinton's foreign policy experience stems mainly from having breakfast at the International House of Pancakes." —Pat Buchanan

---

"He has never been known to use a word that might send a reader to the dictionary." —William Faulkner, on Ernest Hemingway

---

"Poor Faulkner. Does he really think big emotions come from big words?" —Ernest Hemingway, on William Faulkner

"Remarks are not literature." —Gertrude
Stein, on Ernest Hemingway

———•••———

"Literary diarrhea." —Noël
Coward, on Gertrude Stein

———•••———

"I like Wagner's music better than
anybody's. It is so loud that one can talk
the whole time without other people
hearing what one says." —Oscar Wilde

———•••———

"The last bit of methane left in
the intestine of the dead cow
that is post-modernism."
—Robert Hughes, on Jeff Koons

———•••———

"A dogged attempt to cover the universe
with mud, an inverted Victorianism,
an attempt to make crossness and dirt
succeed where sweetness and light
failed, a simplification of the human
character in the interests of hell."
—E. M. Forster, on James Joyce's *Ulysses*

"We don't need refs, but I guess white guys need something to do." —Charles Barkley

---

"They are so unbelievably horrible, so appallingly unmusical, so dogmatically insensitive to the magic of the art, that they qualify as crowned heads of antimusic." —William F. Buckley Jr., on the Beatles

---

"Every word she writes is false, including 'and' and 'but.'" —Mary McCarthy, on Lillian Hellman

---

"In fiction, she is a lady writer, a lady magazine writer." —Lillian Hellman, on Mary McCarthy

---

"How does . . . Francis Ford Coppola, one of the greatest filmmakers of our time, see Keanu Reeves's work, see what we've all seen, and say, 'That's what I want in my movie'?" —Charlie Sheen

"I've seen Don entertain fifty times and
I've always enjoyed his joke."
—Johnny Carson, on Don Rickles

"Reading Proust is like bathing in
someone else's dirty water."
—Alexander Woollcott

"I don't know how Andy can make 60
seconds on *60 Minutes* seem like 60 hours."
—Walter Cronkite, on Andy Rooney

Tip: Cinematic Slams

If you find yourself at a loss for words, why not
borrow from the silver screen? Here are some
classics: "Your mother was a hamster and
your father smelled of elderberries!" —*Monty
Python and the Holy Grail* • "You are a sad,
strange little man, and you have my pity."
—*Toy Story* • "There's a name for you ladies.
But it isn't used in high society—outside of a
kennel." —*The Women*

"Go swallow a bottle of Coke and let it fiz out of your ears." —William Carlos Williams, to Ezra Pound

---

"That turnipy nose overhanging a forward-gaping mouth and hastily retreating chin . . ." —John Simon, on Liza Minnelli

---

"[Mamet's] ear has gone tone-deaf, and his social observations have devolved into clichés." —Frank Rich, on David Mamet

---

"Frank Rich and John Simon are the syphilis and gonorrhea of the theater." —David Mamet

---

"I don't know about the siff, but a theatre without a clap or two would be a pretty lonely place." —John Simon, in reply to Mamet's comment

"Presumably, if you cannot be persuaded to read anything better, Rowling will have to do." —Harold Bloom, on J. K. Rowling's *Harry Potter and the Sorcerer's Stone*

"Somebody should clip Sting around the head and tell him to stop singing in that ridiculous Jamaican accent." —Elvis Costello

---

"I have tried lately to read Shakespeare, and found it so intolerably dull that it nauseated me." —Charles Darwin

---

"The covers of this book are too far apart." —Ambrose Bierce

"A professional amateur." —Laurence Olivier, on Marilyn Monroe

---

"The Detroit String Quartet played Brahms last night. Brahms lost." —Bennett Cerf

Sing Out!

It's always entertaining when artists get upset with critics. Axl Rose called out music journalists by name in "Get In the Ring," off Guns 'N Roses' *Use Your Illusion II*, though fisticuffs never ensued. Taylor Swift had better luck with the 2010's "Mean," apparently written for a specific critic ("All you are is mean and a liar and pathetic and alone in life"). Childish though it may have been, she performed the song at the Grammys to thunderous applause.

Celebs on Physical Attributes

"A bag of tattooed bones in a sequined slingshot." —Mr. Blackwell, on Cher

"I always said Little Truman had a voice so high it could only be detected by a bat." —Tennessee Williams, on Truman Capote

"He looks like an extra in a crowd
scene by Hieronymus Bosch."
—Kenneth Tynan, on Don Rickles

———•◆•———

"Who picks your clothes, Stevie Wonder?"
—Don Rickles, to David Letterman

———•◆•———

"I won't say she's fat, but she had a
face-lift and there was enough skin
left over to make another person."
—Joan Rivers, on Elizabeth Taylor

———•◆•———

"You don't take a sausage roll to a
banquet." —Winston Churchill,
on why he would not bring
his wife on a trip to Paris

———•◆•———

"This person was just brought to my
attention not too long ago. I'm not
quite sure who this person is, to be
honest. I don't know if it is a man
or a woman. I just wasn't sure." —
Christina Aguilera, on Lady Gaga

"Good for her. It's hard for little fat chicks to get anything going."
—Howard Stern, on Lena Dunham and her TV show *Girls*

"We were trying to get pregnant, but I forgot one of us had to have a penis."
—Roseanne Barr, on Tom Arnold

Celebs on Character

"An authentic phony." —James Reston, on Ronald Reagan

"I can still remember the first time I ever heard Hubert Humphrey speak. He was in the second hour of a five-minute talk." —Gerald Ford

"Isn't she a poisonous thing of a woman, lying, concealing, flipping, plagiarizing, misquoting, and being as clever a crooked literary publicist as ever."
—Dylan Thomas, on Edith Sitwell

"So boring you fall asleep halfway through her name." —Alan Bennett, on Arianna Stassinopolous (now Huffington)

"Bob is not authentic at all. He's a plagiarist, and his name and voice are fake. Everything about Bob is a deception. We are like night and day, he and I." —Joni Mitchell, on Bob Dylan

"The *g* is silent—the only thing about her that is." —Julie Burchill, on Camille Paglia

"He is a silk stocking filled with dung." —Napoleon, on Talleyrand

"When they asked Jack Benny to do something for the Actor's Orphanage, he shot both his parents and moved in." —Bob Hope

"Washington could not tell a lie; Nixon would tell the truth; Reagan cannot tell the difference." —Mort Sahl

---

"Mr. Dean appears to be wearing my last year's wardrobe and using my last year's talent." —Marlon Brando, on James Dean

---

"Rock and roll is phony and false and sung, written and played for the most part by cretinous goons." —Frank Sinatra

---

"You have all the characteristics of a popular politician: a horrible voice, bad breeding and a vulgar manner." —Aristophanes

---

". . . An outstandingly unpleasant man, one who cheated and stole from his friends and peed on their carpets." —Kingsley Amis, on Dylan Thomas

"Nobody likes to be called a liar. But to be called a liar by Bill Clinton is really a unique experience." —Ross Perot

—•◦•—

"This arrogant, sour, ceremonial, pious, chauvinistic egomaniac."
—Elliott Gould, on Jerry Lewis

—•◦•—

". . . Personally I consider him a cancer and better removed . . ."
—Axl Rose, on Slash

Where's the Beef?

Nothing's more compelling than a celebrity deathmatch, even if it's fake. When Kanye West and 50 Cent were slated to release albums on the same day in 2007, they trumped up a "beef" to boost sales. The pair appeared on the cover of *Rolling Stone* magazine looking angry, and 50 Cent said he'd retire if West topped his sales. No surprise, it was all a stunt, and though Kanye won the title, 50 is still recording.

"The worst, most dangerous person to America is clearly Paula Deen. She revels in unholy connections with evil corporations . . . plus, her food sucks." —Anthony Bourdain

———•———

"If there's anything disgusting about the movie business, it's the whoredom of my peers." —Sean Penn

———•———

"She's a homewrecker, she is . . . She can rescue as many babies from as many countries as she wants to." —Chelsea Handler, on Angelina Jolie

Celebs on Brains

"He's so dumb he can't fart and chew gum at the same time." —Lyndon B. Johnson, on Gerald Ford

———•———

"[J. D. Salinger is] the greatest mind to ever stay in prep school." —Norman Mailer

"Rock journalism is people who can't write interviewing people who can't talk for people who can't read." —Frank Zappa

———

Lewis Morris: "It is a conspiracy of silence against me—a conspiracy of silence. What should I do?"
Oscar Wilde: "Join it."

———

"It amazes me how someone from your newspaper could ask such a stupid question." —Barney Frank, to Jennifer Steinhauer from the *New York Times*

———

"She's not a bad person, but stupid in terms of gray matter. I mean, I like her, but I like my dog, too." —James Caan, on Bette Midler

———

"Don't be fooled by the dumb blonde routine. This woman is as smart as a rock." —Jimmy Kimmel, on Pamela Anderson

"When your IQ reaches 60, you should sell."

WITH ARDOUR AND ACCURACY

WITH ARDOUR
AND
ACCURACY

The Warrack Lectures on Preaching 1959

by

The Rev. R. LEONARD SMALL, O.B.E., D.D.

St. Cuthbert's Parish Church, Edinburgh

> *He preached and taught about Jesus*
> *with ardour and accuracy.*
> > Acts 18.25 (Moffatt)

THE SAINT ANDREW PRESS

EDINBURGH

Published by The Saint Andrew Press
121 George Street, Edinburgh 2, Scotland
Printed by T. & A. Constable Ltd.
Hopetoun Street, Edinburgh 7
Bound by Henderson & Bissett Ltd
Causewayside, Edinburgh 9

To my Father,
Minister of the Gospel, 1889-1959,
who ever preached with Ardour and Accuracy

FOREWORD

Here is a book on preaching by one of the best-known preachers of our day. To describe Dr. Leonard Small as a preacher might indeed appear to do less than justice to his notable contribution in many other fields to the work and witness of the Church. But an age that is apt too easily to disparage the exposition of the Word needs ever and again to be reminded that still, as at the first, preaching is God's chosen way of arousing the indifferent, reclaiming the fallen, and building up the Church in its most holy faith; and the best possible reminder is to hear again the voice of a born, authentic preacher—and this Dr. Small undoubtedly is. These Lectures are no abstract discussion on the art and science of homiletics; behind them lies the stuff of experience, the actuality of the author's four pastorates, all mightily blessed by God, in Bathgate, Kilmarnock, Cramond, and now in the great parish Church of St. Cuthbert's, Edinburgh. Congregations beyond the seas—in New Zealand and in the United States of America—have also felt the impact of this ministry. It is entirely right that this course of Lectures, delivered originally to Divinity students in training, should now be made available to a wider public; for the proclamation of the Gospel 'with ardour and accuracy' is not to be regarded as the specialised function of a group of men ordained for this task—it is intimately and urgently the concern of all the laity as well. No one will be able to read these pages without being stimulated to fresh evangelism and to a more effective Christian witness.

James S. Stewart.

CONTENTS

7

I

THE NATURE OF THE PREACHER'S TASK TODAY

ANYONE who essays the humbling and challenging task of undertaking to deliver the Warrack Lectures in this day and generation must first stop and give himself furiously to think what is the purpose he is called upon to fulfil, why such a course of Lectures is commissioned year after year, what, to use the terse phrase of current speech, is 'the object of the exercise'? Can it be already, or could it happen in the near future, that here is another of the many foundations established by past benefactors for the benefit of the future, as they sincerely believed, for a long time to come, which have been rendered anachronistic by changing conditions, so that it becomes difficult, if not impossible to carry out the real intention of the original founder. There are many trusts at the disposal of public bodies, and especially Kirk Sessions, for the behoof of the 'deserving poor', laying down conditions and qualifications which in terms of the Welfare State are quite unrealistic, so that action has to be taken in the law courts to alter the conditions, in order that the original intention of the bequest may still be fulfilled. Is this Lectureship like that? Is it in danger of becoming an anachronism? Does the Lecturer's task require to be re-interpreted in order to fulfil the original intention? Surely the answer is both 'Yes' and 'No'. The purpose of giving help to the preacher in his task can never be out of date, so long as God goes on believing in and using what St. Paul called 'the foolishness of preaching' or so long as the Church and the ministry continue to practise that searching but rewarding task. At the same time, every year, with an increasing sense of urgency, that purpose must be directed towards and integrated into the current and contemporary situation. Who, after all, are the 'beneficiaries', if one may use the word in this connection? The Lectures are primarily intended for the students of the theological Faculties of the Scottish Universities. They are not intended to provide a substitute for the theoretical and technical instruction already given in the classes of Homiletics by professors or lecturers appointed for their recognised competence in that specialised field. No, the purpose is to provide additional, direct and practical assistance to men, most of whom are in their twenties, who are going out to the varied work of the ministry, one of whose most exacting, if rewarding tasks is that of preaching; each of whom will have to preach two sermons a Sunday to very much the same congregation, for several years, or even for fifty years, if for one reason or another he follows the old practice of a long ministry in one place. The Lecturer is called upon to speak, if not as a dying man to dying men, at least as a preaching man to men about to preach, who will have to go on preaching, and who will find that Sunday comes round with monotonous regularity, and is on them almost before they realise that Monday is over. Here is the main target, the specific object of the exercise, and all else is incidental. Once printed, they may help the needy, like the hard-driven young minister one saw recently, searching, as blind men seek for light, a little booklet entitled *Starters for Sermons*. They may even cause the theorists, the technicians, the gourmet sermon-tasters to wonder how those who know so little about the real art of preaching can get away with it so long! But all that is beside the point, and to have even half an eye for such is to take one's eye off the main target, the students whom one is supposed to help in their task of preaching. That central emphasis is further borne out by a study of the Lecturers who have undertaken this task over the years. Practically without exception they have been men immersed in the ministry of preaching, exercising that ministry in most diverse situations, from country parish to city pulpit, men like Dr. George F. McLeod, widely known to the vast, scattered, unseen congregation reached by the radio, men like the last Lecturer, Dr. D. T. Niles, famous all over the world as an evangelist, skilled at proclaiming the one Gospel in many lands. In other words, one who is doing the job is asked to give the benefit of his experience to those beginning or about to begin.

If he is honest he will recognise that he is confronted at once in undertaking this task by a difficulty inherent in the task of preaching. He is several years older than, perhaps a whole generation ahead of the students to whom he speaks. He is a product of *his* time, some thirty years ago in the same College, they are the product of *theirs*, and he faces the problem of communication. The students of 1959 were the young children of 1939, their adolescent forming of ideas and ideals, their adult fashioning of beliefs, outlooks and convictions were done in the post-war years, the Korea, Hungary, Suez era, the nuclear-fission Sputnik age. They have been subjected to all the pressures and tensions of their time, all their thinking is subtly conditioned by the mental climate of their day, and if any of them have succeeded in retiring to some ivory tower or finding some private Shangri-La they have had no right to do so, and they will be poorer preachers for it. No one can preach persuasively, powerfully and effectively, who does not strive to understand and enter into the attitude and outlook of his particular hearers, and use every means at his disposal to put his message on their wave-length.

Of course, there is nothing essentially new in this requirement that the preacher should deliberately and conscientiously speak to the condition of his particular people, and translate the essential and unchanging message of Jesus Christ into their language, both of words and ideas. 'The 'modern outlook', as we call it, has confronted every generation of Christian preachers, even if it seems to present to us peculiar difficulties and a stark urgency of challenge. When the writer of the Acts of the Apostles inserted his parenthetical description of the congregation which St. Paul was tackling in Athens, 'All the Athenians and their foreign visitors used to devote their whole leisure to telling or listening to the latest new thing' he was describing the 'current outlook' with which the preacher had to reckon, the mental climate in which he had to work. There is a fine modern 'sough' about these words: 'A hundred years ago, fifty years ago, thirty years ago our fathers were in possession of exact definitions of all the great truths of the Christian Faith. Immense provinces of Christian doctrine were laid down in their theological schemes with all the definiteness and clearness of an Ordnance Survey. Now all this has passed away. The substance of the ancient faith remains, but people find it hard to give their faith a definite expression; and on many questions which seem to be remote from the central truths of the Christian revelation there is the greatest indecision and uncertainty.' What a true description of our modern bewilderment, our sad lack of that 'blessed assurance' of which great crowds have been prepared to sing, at least a whit nostalgically. These words were spoken by the great Dr. Dale of Birmingham in 1880. 'Never before, perhaps, was there the same danger of a wholesale apostasy of the men of mind and culture, not merely from Christianity, but from the religious view of the world.' Someone, surely, said that out of an honest recognition of the mood of the space age, that negative agnosticism or positive unbelief, that 'living as if God were not' which not a few profess and multitudes practise? These were the words of Professor W. P. Paterson at his Inaugural Lecture in the University of Edinburgh, back in the reputedly safe and simple days of the cosy and calcul-able world which existed before the First World War. No, the preacher's situation is not essentially new, although there are in it certain elements of peculiar difficulty of which he must take account, resolutely and resourcefully if he is to exercise with any success or satisfaction the abiding functions of this part of his high calling.

It may be helpful to examine each of these functions

in turn, and seek to relate that part or aspect of preaching to particular elements of difficulty or challenge or opportunity in the contemporary situation.

The first duty for which the preacher is specially commissioned is that of *proclamation*. When Jesus in the synagogue at Nazareth read the passage in which He found the nature of His own commission, He quoted the sixty-first chapter of Isaiah, 'He hath sent me to *proclaim* liberty to the captives . . . to *proclaim* the acceptable year of the Lord'. The great theme of His preaching was proclamation of the Kingdom of God. When He commissioned the twelve we read that He sent them forth to preach, and the word used is *kerussein*, the verb from *kerux*, 'a herald'. Read the first post-Resurrection Christian sermon by Peter in the third chapter of Acts, and it is primarily a proclamation of the great things God has done by raising His Son from the dead and the tremendous consequences that follow. Or turn to St. Paul: the Greek New Testament Lexicon lists fully twenty occasions on which for the words, 'preach', 'preaching', or 'preacher' he uses this word, 'kerussein', 'kerugma', or 'kerux'. The position of the Christian preacher as he mounts his pulpit because Sunday has come round again is essentially that of a herald in ancient days, entering the marketplace to make a public proclamation or a herald of modern days, picturesque survival in his coloured tabard, mounting the Mercat Cross to read a proclamation in the name of the Sovereign or to proclaim a new King or Queen. The herald usually required three things, a trumpet to command attention, a clear voice so that he might be everywhere audible,

and a message worth proclaiming. In a deep sense, and
without straining after effect, we can truthfully say
that these same requirements confront and challenge
any preacher who would speak to the mind and heart
and soul, to the real condition of people today. Men
and women of this generation, young and old, high
and lowly, the intelligentsia and the ignorant, men of
brawn and men of brain are tragically short of clear
convictions and abiding certainties about life in general
and their own lives in particular, about the world they
live in and their own place, value and function therein,
about God, if there be a God, about their destiny under
God and within His purpose, if any purpose there be.
Many of them may try to evade the realisation of this
lack of worthwhile convictions by losing themselves
in the treadmill of the daily round, the common task:

> 'We go to work to earn the cash
> To buy the bread to make us strong
> To go to work, to earn the cash'

and so on, and on, without rhyme or reason, meaning
or purpose. Many more go seeking, seeking after
interest, entertainment, novelty, keeping just ahead and
out of reach of this homesick hankering after meaning,
purpose, certainty, conviction, a faith by which really
to live:

> 'A cradle to cry in, a coffin to lie in,
> Betwixt them I pass through the fun of the fair.
> Fate calling, chance guiding, life's roundabout
>   gliding,
> Until the grey dustman surprises me there.'

Yet no human being can ultimately and permanently evade those issues in life, or escape the eternal mysteries of sin and suffering and death which demand of us strong and steadying convictions and a saving and sustaining faith, or reveal our tragic and utter lack of them. Take just one example of this general rule. How many parents, who have managed so far to handle life, apparently, quite competently, on the basis of their faith in themselves, drawing on their own human resources, are found out when it comes to imparting to their children, in days so bewildering to young people, some sort of faith for living? It is when they go to the cupboard of their own spiritual resources to fetch some real convictions that may be passed on to the sons or daughters whose future means so much to them that they discover their own pathetic, and even culpable bankruptcy. It is to folk like these and to such a condition that the preacher is called upon to speak, proclaiming the facts of the Gospel and the Kingship of Christ. Let him not allow the trumpet to lie tarnished and unused.

No one could complain that there is a lack of cleverness and skill about present-day preaching. Even a perfunctory survey of sermon titles in the Church Notices of any national newspaper will reveal a kaleidoscopic variety of subjects which is positively dazzling . . . though whether it always reveals the glory of God may be another question. There are plenty of men who can handle the free and easy modern style with telling effect, even if their anecdotal adroitness sometimes diverts the mind and soul from the main issue. We are not short of technical knowledge of the preaching art, and there are mechanical aids, all the way from typewriters to tape recorders. What is missing most of all is this trumpet note of proclamation. The old legend tells that some time after Lucifer had fallen from heaven by his own rebellious act he was asked what he missed most, comparing his present condition with his former state. He thought for a little and gave his considered reply: 'I miss the trumpets in the morning'. For all our cleverness and modernity men miss the sound of the trumpets in our preaching, without realising it fully they have a homesick longing to hear it again, and when hear it they do they still respond. Think of the men who have been the giants of the past, Knox, Wesley, Chalmers, Spurgeon. Was there not about the message of every one of them this trumpet note of proclamation, this ring of sheer conviction? Think in our own day of men as diverse as Billy Graham striding up and down the platform of the Kelvin Hall with the microphone in his flowing tie, punching the open Bible with his thumb, or George McLeod broadcasting in the nineteen-thirties 'Govan Calling' or holding forth more recently in the General Assembly on 'Bombs and Bishops'. Do you not hear in each case the trumpet note, and see how men will still listen and respond? Let that note sound through our preaching. Over daily lives that have lost their dignity and grandeur 'trumpeter, sound for the glory of God'. In an age when defeatism in the community and the Church and in all good causes is the most insidious of foes, sound forth the trumpet 'that shall never call Retreat'. There is a department of Apologetics, which has its right and proper function in the

Divinity curriculum, but there is never any excuse for a preacher being apologetic about the facts of the Gospel of Jesus Christ or the triumphs of His grace. Remember, it is almost a physical impossibility to play a prolonged *pianissimo* on a bugle!

What is more, let the voice of the preacher, speaking to real need today, carry clear and true the ring of personal conviction. With an infallible instinct the man in the pew, or the man in the street, will listen for that note, he will be able to tell when it is missing, and he will go away cheated and disappointed, whatever the brilliance of the preacher. What a challenge this is to every man who dares to preach. In the early days of the Oxford Group Movement, Professor Lamont of New College, Edinburgh, returned from a house party to which he had been invited, and made a trenchant criticism of some of the extravagances of the method of 'sharing' to which the guests had been subjected. 'I object', he said, 'to other people emptying the slops of their minds over me.' Harsh, perhaps, but a relevant and valid objection. Any congregation is entitled to object if the preacher whom they have called to proclaim the gospel of Jesus Christ uses his pulpit to empty out on them his doubts and difficulties, his frustrations, uncertainties and bewilderment. If one dared to offer two rules for the preacher who is a product of this particular day and generation, be he angry young man, or just bewildered young man, they would be these: 'Never destroy another's faith, unless and until you have something better to put in its place' and: 'Preach your certainties and convictions, not your doubts and difficulties'. These certainties and convictions may be few, but concentrate on these, preach *them*. An old minister of wide experience said this recently to a group of other ministers, mostly younger than himself: 'As I grow older I find that my beliefs fall into two concentric circles. There is a small circle which contains those beliefs that have grown to be absolute convictions; about them I say no longer "I think" or "I believe" but "I know". It is quite a small circle and these convictions are comparatively few. Outside is a much larger circle containing all that I sometimes believe and sometimes doubt. I would like these things to be true but I am not sure.' 'Of course,' he added with a twinkle in his eye, 'I may still take some more beliefs from the large circle and add them to the central convictions. After all, I'm only eighty-seven!' Here is a sound principle for any preacher. Take your central convictions, few though they be. Preach them, share them with your people; they have doubts of their own aplenty without adding yours to them. Go on adding to these convictions as your experience deepens; then you will have still more to proclaim with the note of truth.

Not least, let the preacher today constantly recover and reaffirm his belief in the worth of the message he has to proclaim. It makes all the difference in the world whether he goes into the pulpit on Sunday, saying within his heart: 'It's Sunday again. I have to say something to these people. What *am* I to say', or realising with fresh wonder every Sunday: 'I have something to say that means more than anything else in all the world to these, my people. How best can I say it?' The preacher of today is called first and foremost to the task of proclamation, he must function as a herald of God.

The second great commission which the preacher must discharge in the setting of conditions peculiar to the present day, and in relation to the modern outlook, is that of preparing the way for Christ to enter, as a living reality, and in saving power, into the whole life of the men and women to whom he is called upon to preach. He is first of all a herald, proclaiming what Christian faith declares to be the facts of the Gospel, the birth, the life on earth, the dying, the rising again, the continued presence of Jesus Christ. He has to make the unshakeable claim that Jesus Christ is the same yesterday, today and for ever, that 'His touch has still its ancient power', that 'faith has still its Olivet and love its Galilee'. Then he must go on to open up a way or ways whereby the Person Who emerges from that story and stands at the centre of that claim may come alive and come home to his hearers. He is a sort of roadmaker for Jesus Christ, whose task and whose glory it is to prepare the way of the Lord. He must survey carefully the nature of the country, the mental and spiritual, the material and economic setting through which he has to prepare this way, the precise nature of the terrain. What valleys have to be exalted, what mountains and hills made low, where has the crooked to be made straight, what rough places must be made plain if Christ is to come into the lives of those that listen? Without overstraining the picture, or over-simplifying the situation, it can be said that the road-maker-preacher must take account of three main features, as real and intractable as if they were physical;

(1) a very large amount of complete ignorance about Jesus Christ and the facts and fundamental doctrines of the Christian faith, like a stratum of hard rock, cropping up and out and revealing itself through the surface of things here and there in the life of all the Churches, and of those on the fringe of organised Christianity as well as among the many completely outside; (2) an occasional, lumpy block of intellectual doubt and difficulty, although these are not as great as one is often led to believe; and (3) constantly recurring and unavoidable stretches of the bog of sheer indifference and complete apathy towards all spiritual issues and everything for which the Christian Church stands. In that situation the preacher, in trying to be a roadmaker for Christ, must very often find himself specialising his craft and skill and becoming a bridge-builder, accepting the function of the priest in ancient Rome, who was named *pontifex*, 'the bridge-maker'.

A bridge is best built, wherever possible, by starting from both sides at once and building out to meet in the middle. The best and most effective preaching is never a one-sided effort, carried out merely from the pulpit, it is a combined operation between the pulpit and the pew, the preacher and the hearer. Whatever the architectural features of the church, the physical and structural arrangements of the building, there is always a 'gap' between the pulpit and the pew which has to be bridged, and it must be admitted that some buildings make this task incredibly hard! The bridging of this gap, entering into rapport with the congregation, winning their co-operation that they may build out from their side to meet him must be the constant concern

21

of the preacher. Establishing that rapport is often a matter of skill, tact, and understanding. Several years ago an Edinburgh minister was sent to a Scottish Border town on market day in connection with a Religion and Life Campaign. He was put in the auctioneer's box in the auction ring with the cattle and sheep producing their own peculiar cacophony of sound on every side, and the hard-headed farmers eyed somewhat askance this preacher in his clerical collar in so unsuitable a setting. He just raised his voice to be heard above the din and said clearly, with a twinkle in his eye, 'Gentlemen, you may think it strange to find me, a parson here in this place. But after all, the event which made me a parson, and created the Kirk and the Gospel took place in just this setting among the animals, where the cattle were lowing.' From that moment he had them, and led them with him unto Him Who was a child in a manger. Cicero called this gift *captatio*, the art of catching and holding the interest and response of one's hearers, and it is an essential part of the equipment of the preacher, who must be roadmaker and bridge-builder for Christ. No sermon is doing what it should if it fails at least to establish a bridgehead for Jesus Christ in some life.

There is one more aspect of the task of preaching in the contemporary situation which must at least be touched upon in this first Lecture before we can go on to consider ways and means whereby the task can best be carried out. A *sermon*, by the very derivation of the name, means 'a talking or conversation with someone'. It is more than and different from an essay read aloud, or even an abbreviated lecture! It must have about it this quality of a person speaking to persons, both collectively and individually, and unless and until each listener receives the impression: 'This man is speaking to me' to that extent and in that respect the 'sermon' fails of its object.

The preacher speaks to his congregation, often, as a teacher speaking to a class, for the need of constructive, coherent and cumulative Christian teaching in our time is clamant. It is to be hoped, of course, that he will not ever convey the unfortunate impression that he is a clever and knowing teacher instructing dull and ignorant pupils! Rather must he persuade his people of his need and theirs to go to school together with the Master Teacher Who is Christ. He will speak, some-times, as the mover of a motion in a debate; he is seeking to win support for the point of view he is putting forward, to persuade enough people to vote for his proposal. 'Like you this Christianity or not?' he will say to them, 'Has it your vote to be true if it can?'. Always, underlying and undergirding the widest variety of topic and treatment, he will speak like a skilled counsel pleading a case before a jury, he is seeking to win a verdict in favour of his Client. He is always appealing for a decision, though he may never in all his ministry make an appeal after the style of the old evangelistic meeting. The preacher has always to rouse men's interest, to elicit their response, to induce their subsequent action. This last is hardest of all. Any devoted and dedicated preacher can make men listen if he speaks with directness, simplicity and sincerity of Christ and the things of the faith. The difficulty is to get them to do anything about it afterwards. In discharging this many-sided part of his task the preacher has to recognise and get to grips with a special problem, more acute now than ever, that is, the inability of the majority of ordinary people to listen and to concentrate. Every teacher knows and laments this problem, and it constitutes a new and baffling challenge to the preacher. When one reads nowadays some of the famous sermons of men like Chalmers, Spurgeon, Talmage, and others of like fame and stature one is left wondering: 'How did men ever listen to these? How did they come to be moved by them?' A generation subtly influenced by the films and radio and television, a generation that has bred teenagers who tell you quite sincerely that they can study better with the radio on, as a sort of background noise, a generation accustomed and expecting to be entertained can never constitute an easy field for the preacher who cannot be content to entertain. In the nature of things every Christian minister must strive in his preaching to persuade people to think for themselves carefully and seriously about life and eternal issues. How can he do that with folk too long 'conditioned' by having their thinking done for them, accepting as 'gospel' whatever is printed in the daily paper they happen to buy, and reading even there little more than the large headlines?

Even so, that is the situation he must accept, the mental climate within which he must operate. It means a constant and deliberate effort to speak the language his hearers will understand, to use the thought-world that can come alive for them, to learn how best he may win and keep their interest that in the end he may produce a real response. That is why he must at all costs teach and preach about Jesus Christ with ardour and accuracy. Accuracy, not only because only truth will serve, only truth is strong and shall prevail, but accuracy also in keeping 'on the beam' and 'on target'. And ardour, most of all, because no cold, detached periods and pronouncements, however polished and finely phrased can get across the essential message of the Gospel in such a situation. The message must be warmed with the fire of a man's own passionate belief, and glow with the heat of his own conviction or no abiding interest will be aroused, no answering spark will kindle, the sermon will not do what it is meant to do. 'That was a good sermon you gave us today Padre,' said the coloured sailor to a U.S. Naval Chaplain on board ship one wartime Sunday. 'Why do you think it was a good sermon, Sam?' asked the Padre. 'You took something hot out of your heart and put it into mine' was the reply. That in present terms, and in face of the modern outlook, *is* a good sermon.

II

THE PREACHER'S MATERIALS . . .
WHAT TO PREACH?

IF proclamation is the note needed amid our modern uncertainty and lack of strong conviction and firm assurance, what, specifically, is a man to proclaim and go on proclaiming over a period of years? If he is to make roads and build bridges along which Christ may travel, to enter into living and saving contact with this congregation to whom he has to preach, what are the best construction materials he can use? If each sermon is to be a talk between persons, a word coming home to the individual heart, what is he to talk about? What message is he to preach with such careful accuracy that it strikes home to the mind and conscience of the hearer with the keen, hard edge of truth? What reality has he to declare with such ardour that he takes something hot out of his heart, and puts it into the heart of the listener? What to preach? . . . there's the question.

First and foremost . . . and this is true in every variety of situation, against the background of every problem . . . *preach Christ.* When a divinity student has completed his training, finished his course and satisfied the examiners, he will be sent forth to preach. To preach what? The jargon of the latest theological school, intelligible or more probably unintelligible to the 'lay' mind to which he must preach, and if the truth were known, quite likely and quite largely unintelligible to himself?

Is he to offer his long-suffering people for their spiritual diet the ill-ripened fruits of his own so-called scholarship, forgetting that most of them have long ago learned lessons about life in the hard school of experience about which, as yet, he knows little or nothing? It does not do to forget that snippets from the lecture notes, taken down, to some degree digested, and then laboriously regurgitated for examination purposes during six years of academic study do not necessarily make for spiritual nourishment and growth in grace in a congregation. No, a man is licenced to preach the Gospel. But what Gospel? The gospel according to Karl Barth, or Norman Vincent Peale, or the school dubbed and decried as 'Fundamentalist', or even, dare one suggest it, the gospel according to the Iona Community? Again, no. The preacher's terms of reference are at once narrower and wider than that. He is licenced to preach the Gospel of Jesus Christ.

That great phrase may be interpreted to mean the Gospel which Jesus Christ Himself preached, or the good news about Jesus Christ, but in either case Jesus Christ is obviously and inescapably central. Here one would enter a strong and urgent plea for more frequent and more definite Christo-centric preaching. That does not mean that every sermon must be 'all about Christ', that His name should be constantly reiterated until the very idea of His greatness and glory and of the sheer wonder of all He has done and does for men has 'died' alike on preacher and hearers out of sheer familiarity. Sermons may and should cover a variety of topics and themes as wide as life itself. On a rare occasion, a particular sermon may not actually use the name of Christ. But every sermon should be Christward directed, wherever it is meant to be going, its navigation should be carried out in relation to Christ and His saving grace, just as an aircraft, flying on instruments only, making constant slight changes of course, climbing, dropping suddenly in an airpocket, flying now in sunshine, now through clouds and thick darkness, is still directed by the response of its precision compass, kept steady through every violent movement, answering the pull of the magnetic north. Thus, a sermon may, occasionally, be on a philosophic theme in the deepest sense, an attempt to think things together and make sense out of them, but all its thinking should be coloured by this double reality, 'No man hath seen God at any time. The only-begotten Son, He hath revealed Him'. A sermon must at times be topical, dealing straightly with some great issue of the moment, like some pronouncement on the vexed question of nuclear weapons. What the preacher has to say on such a problem ought not to be coloured, merely or mainly, by his own political opinions, whatever shade they may be, but rather, compellingly and unmistakably by what he believes about Christ, about His place and power in history, about the new bad conscience He has given and still gives to mankind. A man may well find it laid on his soul and conscience to preach sometimes on subjects that are 'difficult' and not quite 'nice', such as the legislation, currently debated while these lectures were being prepared, for cleaning up vice in the streets of our large cities. Surely no such sermon can be adequate without some reference to our Lord's searching words about the streetwalkers going into the

Kingdom before the 'unco guid' the ultra-respectable folk of His day, and without leaving the final emphasis on His patient and passionate concern for the last, the least, and the lost. A sermon which carries no reference, direct or indirect, express or tacit, to the Gospel Christ preached, or the good news of His salvation, can really be a truly Christian sermon.

Preaching Christ is not only a primary duty, a *sine qua non*, for the Christian preacher, it is also infinitely rewarding.

Nothing else can so successfully and so satisfyingly build up the spiritual life of a congregation, over a period of years, and even through a succession of ministries, each outwardly different. Every minister, not least in his first charge, has to learn to handle a problem of personal relationships which operates in two directions. What is to be his attitude towards his predecessors, and what, at a later date, to his successors, especially his immediate successor? No minister in his first charge should let himself be unduly haunted by ghosts in his own pulpit. He would do better to feel there the uplifting and inspiring Communion of Saints, and remember, for his own challenging, that other men laboured and we are entered into their labours. In the opposite direction it is strange how much easier it is to think kindly about one's successor, once removed, than the immediate successor! If the latter is different from me, with an altered emphasis, another note in his preaching, leaving undone some of the things I did with such enthusiasm, and doing some of the things I know I ought to have done, it is hard for me not to feel, quite unjustifiably, let down, or to wonder how any thread of divine purpose can run through these changes, each man preaching his own gospel, each seeming, somehow, to cancel the others out. Only if each man is preaching Christ, as he sees Him, can this difficulty disappear, and the life of the congregation be continuously built up. A thoughtful and deeply sincere woman, for many years head of the English department in a large secondary school, found herself recently looking back on the half dozen ministers under whom she had sat in succession during the years of this century and delivering this considered verdict: 'Some of these men appealed to the head, and forced one to think; some appealed to the heart, and compelled one to feel differently; one in particular stands out in my memory as appealing equally to the mind and the heart. But the great thing about them all, different though they were, is that every one of them preached Christ.' Preach Christ, and wherever, and to whomsoever God calls you to preach, there you will best serve God's cumulative, continuing purpose of building up that people.

This general statement could be amply borne out by a host of examples. Look at any of the preachers who in any land and in every generation have made their mark, and left not only a name but a lasting heritage behind them. Consider carefully, not those who from time to time rise to popularity like a soaring rocket, circle their little world with coruscating splendour, streaking Sputnik-wise through their particular firmament, sending out their message, be it no more than the characteristic 'bleep, bleep, bleep', only to come down to earth as swiftly as they soared, burnt

out, and soon forgotten without trace; consider rather
the men who, whether as 'popular' preachers in famous
preaching stations, or ministering faithfully for a
generation or more in some quieter corner of the field,
have built to last, left behind a work that has endured
after their own voices were heard no more, and their
personal influence was removed. You will find they
have this common denominator, each and every one of
them preached Christ. Samuel Rutherford in Anwoth,
John Wesley riding to and fro in England, Thomas
Chalmers, and Norman McLeod in Glasgow, Henry
Drummond among the students of last century, and
Billy Graham among their counterparts of our own
day, men as diverse as C. H. Spurgeon and William
Temple, H. E. Fosdick and Reinhold Niebuhr, Joseph
Parker and Leslie Weatherhead, (both in the City
Temple), the scholar-preachers like Denny, H. R.
Mackintosh, W. M. McGregor and Donald Baillie.
. . . they have all preached Christ. Over and beyond all
intellectual gifts, every power of oratory, all developed
and dedicated skill in speaking to the mind and heart
of their particular congregations, that is what lasts.

In this particular connection it may be apposite to
add immediately: 'Preach Christ, and you will be
delivered from the subtle, insidious tyranny of self'.
It was Denny who said: 'No man can at one and the
same time convey the impression that he himself is
clever and that Christ is mighty to save.' These words
may be found framed and hung in not a few vestries;
they might well be so placed in all. It is not at all hard
to understand the story of the famous preacher who
took his eager young visitor to the vestry door and

pointed out the crowd 'scaling' from a packed Evening Service where enthusiasm had run high, and said, 'Young man, there is our temptation'. It is at a different level and in a subtler form that this temptation assails more average mortals. It is so easy to drift, or even to be driven, into the attitude which makes this tacit assumption, 'It is what I say that matters. I have to persuade these people to my opinions, my theology, my slant on things, political, philosophical, practical, personal. I have to fire them with my enthusiasms, share with them my concern, inspire them to love what I happen to love, and to do what I would have them do.' All of which is, of course, in a real sense right and proper, but how dangerously easy it becomes to get self in the centre. Every preacher, however humbling a sense he may have of his own limitations, has his moments when he dreams of preaching to a full kirk and a responsive congregation, and he rightly classes among his real incentives the occasional word of encouragement and appreciation, and even that curiously unsuitable but apparently inevitable phrase: 'I did enjoy you this morning'. The temptation is to measure success or failure in this way and to feel either: 'I am getting somewhere at last' or 'I don't seem to be getting across'. As a companion piece to the words of Denny would not every vestry be the better of offering this constant reminder to the man who is about to enter his pulpit: 'We preach not ourselves, but Christ Jesus the Lord; and ourselves your servants for Jesus' sake'? Amid all the preacher's right and proper efforts after the best effects, his concern with what *he* is going to say and how best to say it, his constant striving to produce the desired impression, he must never lose sight of the ideal, thus expressed by the poet:

> For me 'twas not the truth you taught,
> To you so clear, to me so dim,
> But when you came to me you brought
> A sense of Him.
>
> And from your eyes He beckons me,
> And from your heart His love is shed
> Till I lose sight of you—and see
> The Christ instead.

That is truly preaching Christ, with ardour and accuracy, and with true success.

Preach Christ, and here above all is an inexhaustible subject, an endless theme. There are various theories as to the way in which a man may best exercise his preaching ministry throughout a lifetime of service to the Church extending over a period of forty-five to fifty years. One distinguished former Warrack Lecturer who rose to be Moderator of the General Assembly of the Church of Scotland held a well-developed theory that any man will say, in eight or nine years, everything fresh, personal and distinctive that he has to say, and he had better move on then to another charge and say it somewhere else. He held this doctrine with such conviction that all through his long ministry, like Chaucer's poor Parson 'first he folwed it him-selve'. It is a theory which seems to be coming more and more into favour, yet there are still many men who believe theoretically in, or perforce practise, long ministries. In a country parish in Fife an old minister retired recently, he and his predecessor between them covering no less than 98 years. How can any man go on for nearly fifty years preaching to the same small group of people in a setting that changes little, without running out of ideas and material, and continually repeating himself? He can never come to the end of all that Christ can mean to him and to his people, never utter the last word that can be said about Christ; the sea grows always greater, the horizon keeps dipping away from him, never quite reached; he will never arrive at the point in his own voyage of discovery of the fulness of Christ when like the ancient mariners come to the Pillars of Hercules at the end of the Mediterranean he must cry *ne plus ultra* . . . 'Nothing more beyond'. The preacher, whatever his situation, who goes on faithfully preaching Christ will be delivered from the temptation of perpetually riding his own particular hobby-horse, and the peril of coming back ever and again on what he has said already, until his gospel sounds like an old gramophone record where the needle drops into a well-worn groove, and the record goes round and round, repeating the same words over and over again. 'Unto me', cries St. Paul, 'is this grace given, that I should preach the unsearchable riches of Christ' or, as Weymouth puts it: 'The exhaustless wealth of Christ'. Preach Christ, first and last, and all the time.

Preach the fundamentals of the faith. If it be true, as we have tried to suggest, that this generation is tragically short of clear convictions and positive, firmly held beliefs, then, surely, there is a clamant need for doctrinal preaching. The immediate reaction to this suggestion may be that such preaching is bound to be far too

heavy, much too strong meat for the average congregation, accustomed in other areas of life to being
spoon-fed, and handicapped by that inability to
concentrate to which reference has been made. In
actual fact the so-called average congregation will even
welcome doctrinal preaching as they have not been
prepared to do for some time. Men and women want
to know what, as Christians, they believe, and why
they can still believe it; they are anxious to find truth
which will give back dignity, greatness, meaning and
value to life, truth they can teach to their children
and share with them, so that both they and their
children after them are in a position to give a reason
for the faith that is in them and are not just at the mercy
of the first scoffer who comes along. In the vestibule of
New York Avenue Presbyterian Church Washington
D.C., the Church where the famous Peter Marshall
was Minister, there is one of that Church's most price-
less possessions, an original letter by Abraham Lincoln.
It is housed in a special glass case which cost 2000
dollars, and is dust-proof, rust-proof, moth-proof,
damp-proof, fire-proof and burglar proof! Men do
not want, they can no longer be content in these days
with a faith like that, which needs to be kept in a glass
case. They are looking for a faith that will stand up to
the winds of criticism, and to all the˜pressures of this
modern materialistic world's denials of spiritual values.
The present lecturer has on no less than six occasions,
in three widely differing congregations, and twice in
one (with a decent interval between), as well as in New
Zealand and the United States preached a complete
series of sermons on all the doctrines contained in the

Apostles' Creed, trying to interpret them in the light of present-day thinking, to relate them to the contemporary situation, and rediscover their abiding value and unimpaired relevance. Strange as it may seem, these series of quite deliberately doctrinal sermons, in every case, brought forth more expressions of appreciation of the real help they had given than almost any others. The Rev. David C. H. Read, D.D., formerly Chaplain to Edinburgh University had exactly the same experience with a series of sermons on the great doctrines contained in the Shorter Catechism. *There* are two obvious, ready-made frameworks within which to build up carefully, and over a period, real constructive teaching on the fundamentals of the faith.

Every congregation would benefit from time to time from having a 'refresher course' on the nature and implications of the faith professed, as well as the vows taken by each successive group of young people as they join the Church. 'Do you profess your faith in God as your heavenly Father, in Jesus Christ as your Saviour and Lord, and in the Holy Spirit as your Sanctifier?' . . . these few words cover a range of fundamental doctrine and express an irreducible minimum of Christian truth, and they need constantly to be delivered by fresh study from dying on the hearers through sheer familiarity. Would not every parish minister be the better of preaching about once every year, for the clarification of his own thinking as well as the edification of his congregation, a sermon on the Christian doctrine of Baptism to counteract the common idea of a spiritual equivalent to vaccination, a panacea for every childish ailment; another on the doctrine of Christian Marriage, that it may become much more than a social occasion, 'a good show for Pamela' such as one minister of a fashionable suburban church was asked by the bride's mother to provide; and a third, not the least needed, on the Christian idea of death, burial, resurrection and the life everlasting, that some at least of our pagan thought and practice regarding the final mystery of death may be outgrown?

All this does not mean that the greatest care must not be exercised in developing such a course of doctrinal preaching. Towards the end of last century there came to Kilmarnock in Ayrshire a young man fresh from college, a first-class student, cast in the purely academic mould, and an eager theologian. Very early in his ministry he felt it laid upon his conscience to impart to his defenceless people some of the gems of truth and pearls of knowledge he had acquired in the Aladdin's cave of a divinity college. For a succession of Sunday evenings he inflicted on them 'Proofs of the Existence of God' . . . the teleological proof, the ontological proof, and all the rest that every student knows. After the series had ended the preacher met one of his members on the street, a foreman in a foundry, a real pillar of the Kirk and of the salt of the earth, and was foolish enough to ask the good man's opinion on the sound doctrine thus faithfully preached. The honest man shifted uneasily from one foot to the other, and at last, when pressed for an answer, blurted out: 'Well, Mr. Whitelaw, in spite of all you say, we still believe in God.' Doctrinal preaching, like marriage, is to be entered into 'not lightly or unadvisedly but thoughtfully, reverently and in the fear of God.' At the same time the doctrinal character of the preaching does not need to be laboured or constantly obtruded. H. R. Mackintosh used to say to his students in New College. 'When I shake hands with a man I do not like to grasp a hand limp like a codfish on a slab, I like to feel a man's bones grip through the flesh of his hand. Equally I do not relish shaking hands with a skeleton! So when I hear a man preach I do not like to feel just the bare bones of his theology, unclothed in warm flesh and blood; but I do like to feel the underlying bone structure of his beliefs in every sermon.' Preach the fundamental doctrines of the faith, rediscovering their relevance and applying them in the contemporary situation. After a recent discussion on the radio concerning some modern problem of crime or delinquency, in which there had been much talk by experts about heredity and environment, and free use made of the jargon of modern psychology, a leading official of the British Broadcasting Corporation who never gave any hint of more in the way of religious belief than a detached agnosticism at the best, said to the Director of Religious Broadcasting, 'We can say what we may and be as clever as we choose. Sin, damnation and salvation remain realities.' To these realities the fundamentals of the faith still speak. In such days as these a preacher has no right to be merely toying with the frills of Christianity. He may possibly be able to preach about the 'frills' with some ardour, and by his cleverness arouse some interest; if he neglects the fundamentals he is not preaching about Jesus Christ with accuracy, he is off the target.

Preach, also, from the Bible. Here is another old, long-established emphasis, neglected and decried for a season, and now beginning to come into its own again. Expository preaching, well and skilfully and faithfully done, is of the greatest benefit to preacher and people alike. The wide development of Bible study in recent years is a symptom of a realised need, and of a demand that is becoming ever increasingly conscious and pressing. Ordinary people in the pew, especially those who are bearing any responsibility as office-bearers or as leaders of organisations, particularly among youth, are growing ever more aware that they do not know the Bible as their fathers did, and as they ought to know it, in order to use and apply it. They want to rediscover its abiding relevance and its still living message. That is why the old custom which still prevails in most Churches in Scotland is so deeply and challengingly symbolic. The Service begins with the 'beadle' carrying in the Bible, laying it on the pulpit and opening it before the people. We may say what we like about the architectural atrocities, the ecclesiastical heresy, the practical misplaced emphasis of a central pulpit, the fact remains that at the heart of the traditional Scottish Parish Service is set the preaching, symbolised and interpreted as the opening of the Word unto the people. Preaching that begins from the Bible, that is based throughout on the Bible, that uses a text really as a text and not a pretext, no more than a holy hook on which a man may hang his own words, ideas and pet fancies, destructive or constructive, is of the very greatest value.

The Bible, regard it as we may, as the gradually and

gloriously unfolding story of the revelation of God to men, integrated all the time into man's developing capacity to understand that revelation, always in terms of the thought world and state of knowledge of each progressive stage, or as a Book divinely inspired in a different sense, its every word and syllable, its very punctuation marks and chapter divisions equally sacrosanct . . . however we regard it, the Bible is still the Book of our faith, it is the Book which leads to Christ, Whom we are to preach, from it spring the doctrines we are to teach, it is the living, lasting Word of God we are called to speak and to interpret. There is at once a new demand and a rare opportunity for expository preaching today. Let as strong a plea as possible be entered here for the rediscovery, for this purpose of expository preaching, of that oft-neglected book, the Old Testament. It has become fashionable to decry the Old Testament as a book of battle and murder and sudden death, of immorality and violence, offensive to our refined modern taste and quite devoid of all spiritual uplift. It is time for the preacher to rediscover for himself and introduce his people to the Book that was Jesus' own Bible, for how can the New Testament be understood except against the background of the Old? How rich in preaching material are the great stories which tell of God's forward-moving purpose for Israel and through her for the world, the message of the prophets, sending its challenge ringing down the corridors of the centuries, the poetic and prophetic insights of Isaiah and Jeremiah, to mention only a few of the highlights of this wonderful library of 'Starters for Sermons'. Let any baffled minister, thwarted by the lack of response to general appeals for workers of one sort or another turn to the story of God appearing to Moses at the burning bush. Let him stress the demand for reverence, salutary reminder that when God comes to claim and challenge any man, that must be treated as a solemn and sacred experience. Then let him sketch in the background . . . the miraculous saving of Moses' life as an infant, his upbringing in the royal court giving him a unique inside knowledge, his first hot violent reaction to injustice to a fellow-countryman, and then his cowardly running away, proving he was not yet ready; then the long patient waiting of God during the slow years while the desert silences were deepening and strengthening His chosen leader. From there it is simple to draw the lesson of God's choosing and preparing of men and women still, for every kind of task at every level within His overall plan for His Church in the world. Then the sermon would pass on to the details of the interview; Moses' wholehearted approval of God's intention to intervene on behalf of His enslaved people, followed by the staggering realisation that he, Moses, is to be sent; his excuses, shifts and evasions, like a hunted hare in the centre of a harvest field, and his final outburst of blank refusal: 'Send, O Lord, by the hand of him whom Thou wilt send' or in blunt unauthorised version English: 'Send anyone you like, but don't send me.' Plenty of sub-sections at once suggest themselves. Everyone agrees that the Church's youth work must be continued and further improved; that missionaries must still be sent to other lands, to help build the life of the younger Churches, that it would be a tragedy at home if Church after Church had to be closed for lack of candidates for the ministry; that every congregation must go on finding and supplying responsible leaders and office-bearers, but in all these situations the cause of Christ is crippled because so many reply, 'Send anyone you like, but don't send me.' It will be surprising if that kind of expository sermon, opening up, explaining, applying the meaning of that ancient situation, does not produce results.

Lastly, whatever the nature of the particular sermon, proclaiming Christ, teaching Christian doctrine, expounding the Scriptures, in each and every sermon preach with a sense of urgency to the heart of real and realised need. Principal Martin of New College, Edinburgh, once said to a group of students very near the end of their course: 'Gentlemen, when you are settled in charges of your own, and go into your pulpit of a Sunday you will often be tempted to assume that all these people of yours are happy, contented, prosperous, placid, with hardly a care in the world, and therefore with little real interest in the message you have to give. Always remind yourself that this is quite untrue. Under the surface of their lives are running strong currents of feeling, all the stages and varieties of joy and sorrow are there. Some are worried, some afraid, some utterly distracted by the problems and perplexities, the mysteries of life that perpetually confront real people. Somewhere, in every congregation to which you will ever preach, some heart and soul is crying out for some word of God, which alone can meet that burning need, and you are sent there by God to speak that word.' No truer or more salutary word was ever spoken in connection with this task of preaching. Preach with a burning sense of urgency to the heart of the needs that still cry, often unrealised, from the hearts of men and women. Preach to that need with all the ardour of earnest caring, and preach the whole Gospel of Jesus Christ with all the accuracy and dedicated skill you can bring to bear on the task, and you will find that preaching is infinitely rewarding and deeply satisfying.

III

THE PREACHER'S METHOD . . .
PREPARATION AND DELIVERY

We have insisted that preaching must get back to the Bible, and become once again what it has been so long, traditionally, in Scotland at least, the 'opening of the Word' to the people, a proposition which may seem to many to narrow unduly the scope of their operations,—sticking to the Bible would make them feel 'cabin'd, cribbed, confined'. They want to be left free to draw on the latest best-selling novel, to take as their theme a play like *Look Back in Anger*, to take up and develop from the pulpit some point raised in discussion on radio or television, to preach on 'The Ten Commandments', à la Cecil B. de Mille, rather than à la Moses, or even à la Jahweh! On the contrary, as we shall try to demonstrate in this chapter, a return to the Bible as a source for texts, sermons, ideas, inspiration, can provide a welcome relief and release for the many who have found from experience or realise already in advance 'Me this unchartered freedom tires'. It is not that such novelties are wrong in themselves, indeed their wise and skilful use can be most telling, but the constant search for themes and ideas in such a field can prove devastatingly elusive, and desperation sometimes leads to strange extravagances. Not less exacting and even exasperating to the busy parish minister, disheartened by the daily round, the common task, the

44

fires of his first youthful enthusiasm banked down, if not smothered by what seems to him the complete unresponsiveness of his dull and too-easily contented congregation who have no apparent hunger for any bread of truth he can break for them, may have been the insistence on preaching with a sense of urgency to the heart of realised need. His imaginary example makes it quite clear that it is high time to pass from the realm of declared principle and recognisable and acceptable ideals to that of practice, if these Lectures are to fulfil the 'object of the exercise' and offer some definite and worthwhile assistance to men about to get to grips with 'the foolishness of preaching'.

'How do I set about writing a sermon?' there's the crucial question every young minister has to face as he sits down at his desk or table, virgin-new, or, more probably, secondhand, and stained and rubbed by the labours of some other who toiled at the same un-remitting task before him, with his pen in his hand, or his stuttering, ill-spelling typewriter before him. There is the question which will go on confronting him, week in, week out, with the inexorability of fate, year after year, and, for all our theorising, there is no easy and simple answer. At the same time it may make for clarity and accuracy in such answer as we can attempt, if the task is divided into four stages:

The choice of a subject;

The gathering together of material;

The preparation of the actual sermon;

The method of delivery.

The choice of a subject is obviously of fundamental importance, and demands most careful consideration.

In this connection two main lines of investigation commend themselves as being likely to prove rewarding, just as on a Highland river the ghillie may try one or two different ways of fishing a particular stretch, depending on the conditions of light and shadow, of the wind and the volume of water, for past experience and local lore have proved that these are most likely to work, there, under these conditions. The first encouraging fact to remember and take advantage of is that subjects tend to suggest themselves, with a very little care and encouragement they will almost ask to be preached about. Every minister has had experience at times of a particular theme or text nagging away at his mind and conscience, constantly recurring to his memory, till it positively confronts him, takes hold of him, wrestles with him as did Jacob with the angel, crying: 'I will not let thee go, except thou preach me.' Out of that experience, often, have come most telling sermons, but such experiences must necessarily be rare. At the same time this line of thought can be followed up further. Situations suggest subjects that are relevant, and, indeed, needing to be preached in that context. For instance, a minister in his first charge, as he gets to know and understand his people may find on mature consideration that there are certain aspects of the Gospel, certain implications of the faith, which they have tended to neglect and minimise, there has been an over-emphasis in this direction or that other. A congregation under the influence of a particular minister may have tended to stress a purely private and individual salvation, something that is a matter between the soul and its Maker, but does not concern a man as a husband, wage-earner, neighbour, voter. There may have been too much of what is called an 'evangelical' message, and not enough of a 'total' Gospel, and the balance may need to be restored. Or, again, a congregation may have become too activist, because that emphasis is part of the atmosphere, like the atmosphere of activism which presses so heavily on much of American Church-life, or they may have been forced into this attitude by circumstances, having to make too many efforts to raise money for building or repairs, or, in a new community, being too busy arranging and instituting enough 'things for people to do'. In that situation they may well have neglected the deepening of the spiritual life, and the nourishing of the spirit of reverence and devotion, and a new note must be sounded. None of this is meant to suggest, of course, that any man ever has any sort of right to shew up where his predecessor was wrong, or even by implication to start putting right his mistakes. There was not necessarily anything of that element present in the famous situation when Alexander Whyte and Hugh Black were colleagues in Free St. George's, Edinburgh, and when it was said that 'Whyte blackballed the saints in the morning, and Black whitewashed the sinners in the evening'. It is not so much a case of one man putting another right, as of successive ministries, in the purpose of God and by the guidance of the Spirit, proving complementary to one another and producing in a congregation a more full and rounded and generally satisfying work, witness and worship.

A realistic local situation may well suggest a subject. A time of widespread unemployment affecting a whole area will call for one kind of message, a prolonged period of outward prosperity, producing a subtle, materialistic pagan indifference to the things of the spirit will demand one entirely different. Some tragedy, personal or public, known to and pressing on the heart of a congregation or community will clearly call for some special word from the pulpit spoken in the Name of the God of all comfort. He would be a poor minister who had to search for a subject when he obviously has the chance and the duty to speak with a sense of urgency to such crying need. Then there are all the constantly-recurring special occasions in every congregation; Baptism Sunday with its chance to speak of Christian home and family life; the Youth Parade, with its twofold note of challenge to youth, and realised, shared responsibility divided between the home, the school, the church, the youth organisations; an Ordination of Elders with the opportunity to speak of our debt to Christ and our dedication to His service, —on these and a dozen other such special occasions we find the minds and hearts of our people turned already in a particular direction, and it is well to seek a text, a Bible incident, a subject which will make it possible to speak a special word from God relating to that particular occasion. How often a glorious chance is missed in this respect.

In this connection an obvious suggestion to make is the observance of the Christian Year. What better way is there to proclaim Christ, continuously and coherently, than by following the events of His life as they occurred; what more thorough course of teaching can be given in the fundamentals of the faith, how better can one

48

use the Bible for preaching purposes than by following in it and retelling from it the story of the life and death and rising again, and the growing Church of Him to Whom the whole Bible points? Here is a whole series of subjects, great in themselves and inexhaustible in the depth of their abiding meaning and relevance.

It is a great pity, however, if preaching becomes merely or mainly *ad hoc*, and that may well be the severest defect of preaching in our time. For the true edification of the Church, the steady building up of the life of a congregation, more is needed. Multiply the special occasions as we may, and use their every specialised opportunity how we will, there remain long stretches of ordinary weeks; there are far more 'Low Sundays' than the one so designated in the calendar. It is for them that the practice of preaching courses of sermons can be recommended. Mention has already been made of courses of doctrinal sermons on 'The Apostles' Creed' or the vows of Church membership, but this same principle can be much more widely applied. For teaching and exposition, what about a course on the Beatitudes, treated as 'Christ's own Secret of true Happiness', or any part of the Sermon on the Mount, its searching challenge realistically applied in the modern situation? The Parables are an unfailing source of inspiration and carry still their own unchanging message. One has heard a most instructive series, dealing with the sayings of Jesus beginning 'Verily, verily, I say unto you', and entitled 'Jesus stresses a Point'. An honest and careful study of the healing miracles in the light of modern medical and psychiatric practice, seeking to understand

D 49

and interpret what Jesus did for each 'case' rather than to explain away the miracle, might be called: 'How Jesus healed and heals' and could not fail to win a hearing in this generation which suffers from such divers diseases of body, mind or spirit, or all three together. Or, for a change of emphasis and approach, what about 'People Jesus Met', following, say Luke's Gospel, so rich in graphic description of incidents and character, beginning with Simeon, the old man who kept his dreams, and going on through Matthew the taxgatherer, Simon the Pharisee, Jairus the ruler of the synagogue, the Roman centurion, the family at Bethany, by way of blind Bartimeus and Zaccheus to Simon of Cyrene and the penitent thief? In the *Acts of the Apostles* there is the whole fascinating story of the early growth of the Church, so challenging in its reminders of the essential qualities of a living Church, people waiting together on the Spirit, worshipping, working, witnessing together, and the ways in which the Gospel spread when it first burst the bonds of Judaism. Turn to the Epistles and hear how the needed note of certainty and conviction could be sounded with a series on 'Trumpet Tones of Truth' with texts such as: 'I know that the sufferings of this present time are not worthy to be compared with the glory which shall be revealed', 'We know that all things work together for good to them that love God', 'I am persuaded that neither death nor life . . . shall be able to separate us from the love of God which is in Christ Jesus our Lord', 'I can do all things through Christ which strengtheneth me', 'My God shall supply all your need according to His riches in glory by Christ Jesus'.

Nor, recalling what was said earlier, should the Old Testament be neglected. What rich veins of precious metal remain here, nothing like worked out, after all these centuries. More than one course of sermons could be preached on, say, 'Dramatic Scenes from the Old Testament'. . . . Abraham with the knife poised for the downward stroke that will kill his only son, and cut the thread of God's purpose and promise for the future . . . how stark we see the hard obedience God asks of His servants, how ringing clear the question: 'Beyond what point is it I am not prepared to go in trust and faith?', and always, in the background the thought: 'He that spared not His own Son'. Jacob and Esau meeting again after all these years, with so much between them of bitter wrong inflicted and suffered, Jacob and his family utterly at Esau's mercy, a rare, long-dreamed of chance to visit the sins of the father on the children; Esau's quiet, dignified magnanimity: 'I have enough my brother' . . . what a story to make real the truth so many congregations sing sentimentally and unthinkingly: 'All for sin could not atone'; what a chance to describe this scene alongside the picture of the returning Prodigal, the 'how much more' of God's forgiving love; what an opportunity to breathe the breath of life into the too-familiar phrase: 'Forgive us our trespasses, as we forgive them that trespass against us'. Or, in similar vein, what of the picture of Joseph, mighty man of power in Egypt, when his chance came after their father had died and there was nothing to prevent him exacting revenge from the brethren who were responsible for all the ills he had suffered, answering their cringing appeals to be spared their deserts with these noble words: 'As for you, ye thought evil against me, but God meant it unto good to bring to pass as it is this day to save much people alive.' What a chance to make real a belief after which so many are groping today, the doctrine of an over-ruling providence that can make good come even out of evil, can weave even our sin and failure into a pattern of blessing, can make even the wrath of men to praise God. So one could go on and on, through the scene where Nathan the prophet tells David his story of the rich man and the poor man's one ewe lamb, till David's anger kindled against the man who had done this heartless, wicked thing. Then swift, like a dagger to the heart, comes the prophet's pointing finger, and the whole essence of the story 'Thou art the man'. Is there ever any congregation where a sermon with that emphasis does not need to be preached at least once a year? Dr. Fosdick quotes the entry which Longfellow made in his diary on Sunday, August 5th, 1860, 'John Ware, of Cambridge, preached a good sermon. I applied it to myself'. Would it were ever, or at least oftener, thus! One other instance only . . . the contest of Elijah with the priests of Baal on Mount Carmel, when Elijah calls for this dramatic trial of strength between the rival claimants for the loyalty of his people and cries: 'How long halt ye between two opinions? If the Lord be God serve Him, but if Baal then serve him.' There is a good Scots word which sums up this challenge 'stop swithering', and seldom has that challenge been so badly needed by so many so often as it is today. The Old Testament abounds in such scenes with a clear and living message.

Then there are all the possibilities in the Great Texts from the Old Testament. The grand opening phrase of the whole Bible: 'In the beginning God'; the searching, succinct definition of man's essential nature: 'Man became a living soul'; ringing notes of encouragement like the re-iterated message to Joshua: 'Be strong and of a good courage'; depths of human feeling, like David's lament for Absalom: 'Would I had died for thee, my son, my son'; these and many more truly great texts maintain their unchanging influence. And what of all the great words that almost sing themselves now in the minds of us all, because they are wedded in indissoluble union to great music? John Newton, famous as composer of grand hymns like 'Glorious things of thee are spoken' and 'How sweet the name of Jesus sounds' preached no less than forty sermons on the words set to the music of Handel's *Messiah*. Here, again, is an endless store of possibilities.

One more line of approach must at least be indicated. The message of the prophets has an astonishing and stimulating relevance to present conditions and will reward careful study and skilful re-interpretation. No man can avoid preaching a 'total' gospel once he starts declaring the message of Amos, with his series of woes upon the nations, coming right home to his own people, and his flaming denunciation of social injustice in every form. Even a modern suburban congregation, though they may not actually drink wine in bowls, or lie on couches of ivory, ought not to find Amos dull! A generation which has seen so many broken homes, and such tragedies of infidelity, should be 'tuned in' to Hosea's great message, born of his own bitter experience with his worthless, faithless wife, concerning the love that will never let us go, never give us up.

This mention of the prophets may serve to illustrate a danger which must constantly be guarded against in all this use of courses. Dr. Harry Millar, whose great work in the New College Settlement in the slums of Edinburgh will long be remembered, and who spent the last years of his life as Principal of St. Mary's College, St. Andrews, used to tell how he returned on a visit to his first Church at Largo, and began to exchange reminiscences, as men will, of this and that with his old beadle. A twinkle came into the old man's eye. 'Do ye mind,' he asked, 'yon series of sermons you gave us on the Minor Prophets, soon after ye came to Largo?' 'Yes, I do indeed,' replied his now famous former minister, delighted (as who would not be?) that his youthful preaching had left so indelible a mark. 'Man,' chuckled the beadle, 'yon was extraordinar' dry!' No course must last too long, and a keen sensitivity must note when it has ended its usefulness, but any such course has two advantages, as Professor Emil Brunner used to point out to his students in seminar. You are delivered from the endless, and sometimes desperate search for a text and a subject; you know where you are going next, and, especially if you are following a course of expository sermons, your people know too; when you have finished, both you and they know where you have been. Not less important is the fact that certain subjects, otherwise ticklish and difficult, will come up inevitably; your people will realise this and accept the situation. If you are preaching on the Ten Commandments you must speak on 'Thou shalt not kill' and topics as diverse and controversial as capital punishment and the use of nuclear weapons are bound to come up. If you are going through the Sermon on the Mount you will come naturally and inevitably to the section about the commandment against adultery and the deeper importance of wrong desire; you will have to deal with the Christian attitude to the whole difficult subject of sex, and your people will expect you to deal with it and not shirk the issue. Handled wisely, the use of such courses can be of the greatest assistance, to preacher and people alike.

Once the subject is chosen, and the text selected, the gathering of the material begins. Begin with the text, studying it in its context, seeking to get to the heart of its meaning, which is the least that must be done if we would avoid the danger of 'handling the word of God deceitfully', reading into it what we want, rather than opening it and letting out its meaning. Go back if possible to the original; that, after all, is presumably why Hebrew and Greek are still necessary evils in the divinity curriculum! It is often most rewarding, and there are shades of meaning not brought out in any translation. For instance, the word translated 'troubled' in the first verse of the fourteenth chapter of John is the word that would be used of the water of a loch, whipped into short steep waves by the wind sweeping down the glen, or the seething, tumbled waters where two tides meet among the Western Isles. The word in Martha's appeal to Jesus 'bid her that she *help* me' is the word for 'taking hold of a burden along with someone else', like taking a pull on a rope, or lifting the end of a stretcher. At the very least, use a good commentary, which does not mean lifting shamelessly whole sermon outlines from a commentary. Often a helpful suggestion will be found in another translation, say, one of the many modern versions. Set alongside the lovely words: 'Thy gentleness hath made me great' this splendid version: 'Thine answers to prayer have raised me'. Match the lyrical associations of 'I know that my redeemer liveth' with this flourish of trumpets: 'I know one to champion me at the last, to stand up for me on the earth.' Versions in other languages can add their quota of helpful ideas. The German Bible has in Psalm 23 'Er erquicket meine seele' . . . 'He quickens my soul', while one of the French versions of the Beatitudes has 'Les artisans de la paix', 'The artisans of peace', not the people who talk about peace, nor the experts who plan it (not with conspicuous success) but the workmen who make it.

Counsels of perfection would be that after letting Monday lie fallow, as far as one is ever allowed to do so, Sunday morning's text and subject, at least, should be chosen on Tuesday, and the preliminary spadework done. Thereafter, to mix the metaphor unashamedly, the theme and ideas can be left to 'simmer' for a little. Ideas relating to the main theme will begin to suggest themselves. Trains of thought will begin to link up, then illustrations will come. They will seldom come 'like some bright dream that comes unsought', they will need to be looked for, tracked down, dug out. But from where? Here some consideration must be given to the whole vexed question of the use of illustrations. The use of them can be overdone, as in the case of the busy final-year student assistant who told his friend that his sermon was almost ready: 'I've got three grand illustrations. All I need now is a text'. An illustration must illustrate and not merely distract the hearer's attention; it must not leave him so intrigued, amused, or even startled by the illustration that his attention is diverted from the point at issue; a good illustration will focus attention not on itself but on the truth it is meant to make more clear; the final test of a good illustration is this . . . after the Service is over do people remember only the illustration, or the point it illustrated? Beyond all question the telling use of illustrations is most effective, especially with a modern congregation whose powers of concentration are limited, and whose interest needs to be caught and often recaptured. Even humour, surely, has its proper place and function. Jesus used it in His preaching, for He could not have spoken of the beam and the mote, or the Pharisee, straining a midge out of his soup and swallowing a camel, without a twinkle in His eye and a smile on His lips. Of course, it can be overdone; and the man who 'has them rolling in the aisles' is not likely to be dealing very successfully with the fundamentals of the faith, and will soon pall; caviare may be piquant and tasty as a change, but as a staple diet it leaves much to be desired.

Where can one find good, apt, telling illustrations? From three main sources, reading, observation and experience. Reading of the widest variety, but especially biography, and not least the story of lives lived out within living memory and in our own day and generation is a most fruitful source of helpful illustrations. So likewise is observation. For a recent TV programme on the Service of Confirmation at which young people were admitted to the Church a photograph was taken of the particular Church in which the service was to be held. When it was enlarged someone noticed that right in the forefront just beside the Church gate was a road sign 'Road Narrows'. What an excellent illustration of the fact that for these young folk the road had narrowed to the point of decision and committal, and someone had observed it. Personal experience is the most obvious source of all, but it must be used with the greatest care. One's own pastoral experience abounds in such illustrations, but references to real people must be carefully disguised, and confidences most strictly observed. As a mere matter of mechanics it is wise to keep a notebook for good illustrations, with at least an indication of where they may be found again when they are wanted.

After the materials are collected comes the task of actually preparing the sermon. Apart from the rare man who is peculiarly gifted the vast majority of us for our own good and the benefit of our people had better accept the old convention of always writing something, at least, whether the whole sermon, fairly full notes, or careful headings and sub-headings. The men who never set anything down, who have it all planned, just in their own minds or enjoy working out the argument as they go along, generally end up, if they stay long enough in the one charge, by repeating themselves, adopting certain personal cliches, weaving patterns of words, words. The extreme case of this tendency is the famous story of the visiting evangelist, conducting a mission in a certain town. The local

minister who was 'Chairing' the meeting asked the
preacher just before going into Church what particular
lesson he would like read. The answer was blandly
given, 'It doesn't matter . . . I have no idea what I am
going to say until I stand up to speak. I shall say what
the Spirit gives me to utter'. The poor pedestrian
parish preacher replied, a shade drily, 'I find it more
profitable to wait upon the Spirit earlier in the week'.
No man has a right to offer to God and set before his
people a piece of work, shoddy, slovenly, and ill-
prepared, to bring into the pulpit anything less than
the best of his specialised training, native endowment
and developed ability and call that being truly spiritual.
An expert in another field, a successful novelist may
serve as a guide here. He writes: 'The first thing is to be
aglow with your subject. A scene, a plot, a character,
fires the mind emotionally, lays hold of you, and you
are aflame with your subject. You cannot write until
a thing takes you like that. Now I take the inspiration
and I set it all down in hot, palpitating words, crude,
rough, unexamined sentences—words that come without seeking. Then I tuck up my sleeves and begin. I
work with mechanical care, subjecting all to cold
scrutiny, keeping feeling in control, and letting all my
critical faculties full out, and as I work I recover that
fire, chastened, restrained, but with new power
because of restraint.

It generally comes at the fifth time of writing.'

Counsels of perfection, indeed!

In passing, it may be noted that there are certain
mechanical aids to meticulous preparation for those
who have the money to buy them and the time to

employ them. It is known for a preacher to preach his sermon in advance into a tape-recorder, and then play it back, and in certain of the Divinity Colleges in the U.S.A. a student sits in a room fitted with close-circuit television, so that while he practises his sermon Burns' famous aspiration is for him fulfilled: 'O wad some po'er the giftie gie us, tae see oorsel's as ithers see us'! One cannot help wondering whether such gadgets are not apt to produce a certain self-conscious concentration on technique, and to leave the main question in the preacher's mind, 'How am I doing?'

Even more important than such polishing of technique should be a constant concern to translate the message into the speech and the thought world of the particular congregation. The preacher may not realise it but he is regularly confronted with a problem akin to that faced by the experts who seek to translate the Bible or portions of it into some new language. Missionaries in Greenland had to translate 'the Lamb of God' into 'the little white Seal of God' for people who had never seen and could not picture a sheep. In one of the dialects of the East there was no word for 'love' and no word for 'God', so 'God is love' had to become 'The Great Spirit is not angry' . . . a poor substitute. A tribe of nomads in the centre of the Sahara had to be told 'We have hope . . .' not 'as the anchor', but 'as the picketing-peg of the soul' . . . different words, same idea. In the same way the preacher has to translate his message into terms that are real to men who know all about carburettors and camshafts, but to whom words like 'grace' or 'repentance' have lost their meaning and to women who are familiar with washing-machines, and bleaches and detergents, but to whom 'sanctification' means exactly nothing. Billy Graham's story applies to parish preachers who just have to go on and on, as much as to visiting evangelists who come and go. He tells of a friend who went by air to fulfil a preaching engagement in the College Chapel of a big town out West. When he got over the town there was a thick fog and the plane could not land. 'There were the congregation, all waiting down there in the chapel:' said Billy, 'And there was the preacher going round and round in the fog over their heads, and he couldn't get down'. Not the least part of sermon preparation is a constant, painstaking concern to get down.

So comes the final stage, the delivery of the sermon. Here every man must develop his own method and work out his own salvation. Some read closely, which is a little difficult to do effectively and unobtrusively. Yet Chalmers read every word, even following the words along the line with his finger, but as he went on he caught fire, and the fire kindled the heart of the hearer. Some commit a carefully written sermon to memory, a process formerly known as 'mandating'. This can prove a great strain, and can become a subtle form of cheating, as it conveys the impression that the preacher is speaking 'freely' when he is really reading it, though only off the back screen of his mind. Some work from notes as a guide, without ever obtruding the fact; others, having prepared with very real care, can speak without notes. To each man the method which, by trial and error, he has found to work best with himself! Whatever the method there remain two indispensable prerequisites, and they are contained in the general title of these lectures, ardour and accuracy. A typical moderate's sermon more than a century ago was described as being like an autumn day, short, clear and cold. Coldness is still fatal. If a preacher is detached and cold, if his pronouncements are not fired by his own convictions, if what he says is not warmed by what he passionately believes he will win and convince no one. On the other hand he must not be all warmth, degenerating into what has been described with deadly accuracy as 'havering earnestness'. There was sheer inspiration behind the printer's error in setting type for the thirteenth chapter of First Corinthians, 'Though I speak with the tongues of men and of angels, and have not clarity'. To speak so that we are clearly heard, to preach so that we are clearly understood, to strike a spark of fire in some answering heart, let that be our aim and ideal in preparing a sermon.

III

THE RELATIONSHIP OF PREACHING
TO THE REST OF THE PREACHER'S
FUNCTION

How is adequate sermon preparation to be worked in with all the other necessary duties of the average Parish Minister?

First and foremost, it is of paramount importance to observe a scale of priorities, and to keep revising and renewing it constantly. Time, energy, health, optimum efficiency are all strictly limited, and no man can possibly do everything that he might like to do, or that others may expect him to do. In addition to his obvious duties as preacher and pastor, if one's own experience is any guide, the minister may be called upon to serve on community and church committees, to take a responsible part in youth work, both inside and outside his congregation, to be a school chaplain and an industrial chaplain, and to take a large share in promoting all good causes within the community, especially if it is a comparatively small community, in a country or rural area. In the larger towns and cities, where congregations are generally bigger and more highly-organised, the problem is accentuated. Some thirty years ago Emil Brunner would tell his students in Zurich that the minister under modern conditions was expected to be a kind of business executive, functioning more and more as an organiser and administrator, and less and less as a preacher and pastor. What he would say, now, under present conditions, one dare not guess. Perhaps this tendency may be seen most clearly in the United States where it has gone infinitely further, in terms of much larger whole-time staffs, and far wider use of modern equipment and techniques than we could attempt or even dream of in this country. Personal experience of American Church-life from the inside has left one filled with admiration not unmixed with envy, but also with the firm determination to resist the demands and the problems inherent in over-organisation. Brunner's contention in the context of Church life thirty years ago is more than ever cogent today, on both sides of the Atlantic. We are trained, called, and ordained, first and foremost to be preachers of the Word and pastors of men's souls. The traditional wording of the preamble to a Call in the Church of Scotland is a sacred and solemnising reminder of this essential emphasis: 'We . . . being assured, by good information and our own experience of the ministerial abilities, piety, literature, and prudence, as also of the suitableness to our capacities of the gifts of you. . . . Minister of the Gospel, . . . do heartily invite, call and intreat you to undertake the office of Pastor among us, and the charge of our souls.' Nothing could be plainer or more challenging; these, and none other, are the terms of our remit, and nothing whatsoever must be allowed so to invade the area of the minister's work as preacher and pastor that this two-fold function, which is specifically and peculiarly his, becomes ever anything less than unmistakably central. The Church, not least the Presbyterian Church, functions through committees, and it is only through service on committees very often that a man can fulfil his ordination vow to play his due part in the affairs of the Church, both in the local and the wider sense. It is cheap and easy to decry the work of committees; like the much-maligned Martha we would be poorer without them at their best. At the same time, in the interests of keeping a sense of proportion, it may be worth setting on record the following definition of a committee, taken from the walls of a committee room in London, 'A Committee is a collection of important people who, individually, can do nothing, but, collectively may decide that nothing can be done'. No amount of service on committees, however important the committee, and however responsible or distinguished the service rendered, can excuse a man for neglecting, save on rare occasions his primary pastoral duties, or scamping his pulpit preparation. This whole committee business can become like the notorious tide-rip-cum-whirlpool of the Corrievreckan, off the West Coast of Scotland—once let a man get drawn into the vortex and he cannot get out. It is a little tragic when any minister can claim with pride, not untinged with sadness, but still pride, that he serves on twenty-two committees! This is a question not just of rights and wrongs, but of priorities.

In most communities and congregations the life of the organisations, particularly among the young, requires constant interest and frequent nursing. Very often the minister himself must act as a leader, and this is, in itself no bad thing, forming a most useful extension and application of his parochial ministry.

Just because he has got to know his young folk and they have come to know him amid the fun and games of the Youth Club or the Youth Fellowship Party, or in the shared fellowship of Scout or Boys' Brigade camp, he may be all the better able to lead them into the deep things of the faith. But, again, let all things be done within reason, and let the balance be maintained. In his right and proper emphasis on youth, let not the pastor neglect the old folk who are also his care, or give them any justification for saying: 'He isn't interested in anyone over the age of thirty' (they will say it anyway!). In his concern for a multiplicity of organisations, all needing to be kept in a healthy state, let him not forget that the Church is an organism, and that he has a peculiar responsibility, by his faithful, careful preaching of the Word, for maintaining the living connection between that part of the body which is his Church and the Head, Who is Christ.

The witness of the minister within the community is regarded, in our day, as being of the very greatest importance, and rightly so, and here every minister should be giving a lead to and setting the pace for his people. He may well be prepared, and surely should be on occasion, to divert time and energy from the care of the flock already gathered to go out after the wanderers and the careless, quoting, quite justifiably, 'the ninety and nine that safely lay', all the more so as the percentages are now so different from 99 to 1. Yet again he must watch the emphasis. It will not do for a man to be so busy going to and fro in the earth (like a certain none too illustrious example in the Prologue to the Book of Job) evangelising the whole country, that he leaves too long and too often untended the corner of the vineyard for which, under God, he is directly and specifically responsible. If a man's soul and conscience so direct him, then let him play a declared and committed part in politics, allying himself to this or that policy or party; but let him also watch lest the man in the street and even the man in the pew come to think of him as 'the Vice-Chairman of the Ward Labour Party', or 'the Convener of the County Education Committee', or 'the Provost' whatever the colour of politics of the local Town Council, rather than 'the Minister'. Keep carefully and conscientiously a true scale of priorities, and overhaul it frequently.

Even when the minister's function as preacher and pastor is kept, deliberately and with difficulty, thus central, a conflict still remains. Which is he to be, first and foremost, whenever a choice has to be made, preacher or pastor? Where is the greater part of his time to be spent? On the roads, and the stairs and in the homes of his people, or in his own study, with his books and his sermon preparation? Sometimes the conflict is drawn in artificially sharp lines. It has been said that no man can be with equal emphasis and ability at one and the same time a good preacher and a faithful pastor, and each must choose one or the other, according to his gifts and inclinations. Either way a man lays himself open to the obvious temptation of doing what comes more easily to himself, and shirking the healthful discipline of tackling conscientiously that which is difficult. But, surely, this whole sharp antithesis is artificial? Though one man may be more naturally a pastor, at home with people and personal issues, than a preacher, in his element handling words and ideas, he must still preach the best way he can to be a real shepherd of souls; and though another may feel he is fulfilling his appointed destiny by clothing in well-chosen words the word God has given him to speak from the pulpit, he is still responsible for the pastoral care of all his people, not least those who, for one reason or another, cannot or do not ever come to hear him preach. Since these are Lectures on Preaching and not on Pastoral Theology, let us tip the balance of our chosen emphasis on the side of this statement, bald and provocative as it may seem at first sight: 'The preacher who maintains a fair balance between the pastoral care of his people and careful pulpit preparation, will in the long run, and over a period make a better preacher'. Now, why?

Let us go back and take up again a few points made earlier. In outlining the precise nature of the preacher's task in relation to the contemporary situation and the modern outlook his function was compared to that of a road-maker for Christ, and even more specifically a bridge-builder. Particular emphasis was laid on the necessity for bridging the gap between the pulpit and the pew and persuading the hearer to build out from his side of the relationship his own response, so that he is not merely passively receiving the message of the preacher, but entering into active and positive co-operation with him. Where the man in the pulpit is already known to the people in the pews, as the pastor they see on other days than Sunday, going in and out of their homes on the many and varied duties of an under-shepherd of Christ Himself, sharing in their joys and their sorrows, with them on the red-letter days and the dark days, and even on the drab, grey ordinary days which make up so much of life, then they will be 'with' him even before he starts to preach, the essential rapport between pulpit and pew will already be established. What a great day when that point is reached and realised in the relationships between minister and people! The solemn, heart-searching Service of Ordination and Induction is over. He and they have sung from opposite sides of the newly-established relationship, the words of the Ordination Hymn:

> Wisdom and zeal and faith impart,
> Firmness with meekness, from above,
> To bear Thy people on their heart,
> And love the souls whom Thou dost love.
>
> To watch and pray, and never faint;
> By day and night strict guard to keep;
> To warn the sinner, cheer the saint,
> Nourish Thy lambs and feed Thy sheep.

What a programme for any man these old words outline. The days pass, and the Sundays come, and the people remain largely unknown, anonymous faces, seen from the pulpit. Then, bit by bit, he gets to know them; he can put names on more faces every week, sees a particular situation behind each recognised face or family; till one day comes the dawning realisation, these are really his people, he knows them, and they know him, they look to him for leadership and he can look to them for loyalty. And how deeply rewarding and satisfying to look back in after years and know it has been so. Every minister of experience will agree that when he goes back to visit a congregation where he formerly ministered it is always certain types of people who come round to the Vestry to shake his hand and renew acquaintance . . . couples whom he married, or whose children he christened, former invalids whom he visited faithfully in hospital, people into whose homes he went at a time of tragedy or bereavement as the messenger of the God of all comfort . . . in other words people who were bound to him by ties of some personal pastoral relationship. It is such special relationships which, in retrospect, make all the daily round, the common task, of pastoral care so rewarding and worthwhile, and the forging of such personal bonds is the very minimum that any man may require of himself, if he is to take his duties as a pastor seriously at all. But the man who, not content with visiting his people in illness or bereavement, and sharing with them only such special joys or sorrows, seeks by the faithful, systematic shepherding of his flock to increase continuously the area of such personal contact, not least with the seemingly careless and indifferent, puts himself in a position of great advantage. Not that this is easy, but it is more necessary than ever. By a queer law of topsy-turvy mathematics the larger the congregation, and the more widely scattered its membership, the more difficult it is for the minister to keep touch with them, and at the same time the more important it becomes to maintain this personal contact between the preacher-cum-pastor and the people. The man who succeeds in this exacting task, and does not simply give up the unequal struggle, starts every sermon with a wonderful advantage; the bridge is built already, he and his people are together before he starts.

It was further suggested that a 'sermon', by the root meaning of the word, should be like a personal conversation, a man speaking with his friend. It requires therefore to be expressed, consciously and carefully, in whatever language the hearer is best able to understand. If you had to speak regularly to a person who is deaf and dumb, you would perhaps take the trouble to learn the deaf and dumb language, or if that person could lip-read you would enunciate slowly and distinctly so that your conversation might be understood. When a new missionary arrives in an overseas field he may not be allowed to start preaching for six months or a year, however badly his preaching gifts may be needed, for he must first learn the language thoroughly. It is only by living among the people, entering into their thought world, quite different from his own, picking up the local idiom, that in the end he can do his message justice, and really 'get it across'. That need confronts every preacher, and there is a very real difficulty here, greater than is usually recognised. During the War a member of a Glasgow congregation, whose minister would be generally regarded as a 'popular' preacher, began to compile a list of words which the minister used and which had lost their meaning for the average hearer or meant to him something different from what the minister implied. For instance, this was at the time of the fall of Tobruk and the word 'surrender' went down on the list, for, argued the compiler, the minister talked about 'surrender' to Jesus Christ as something fine and desirable, whereas to the ordinary man it meant something rather disgraceful. He got up to a list of 300 words! Even if one writes that off as being too captious for words, the underlying theory was valid. The greatest care must be exercised to use in preaching the right words to convey to these particular hearers the desired shade of meaning. Once again, a parallel situation is to be found in the task of translating the Scriptures into native tongues. The pitfalls for the unwary are sometimes weird and wonderful. One translator in West Africa worked out what he thought was a good word to translate the phrase 'to save', which is at the very centre of the Gospel message. For years he went on using it, only to learn at last that it meant merely keeping ragged clothes together. His hearers were all too polite to tell him! On the other hand a little inside knowledge can suggest the exact right word on occasion. Living among the Navajos another translator found that they had a very telling phrase for our word 'worry'. They would say, 'My mind is killing me'. What a perfect description! It is by living and moving among his people, entering into their homes and daily lives, understanding how they think and speak, what are their hopes and fears, the realities of life to which so often the message of the Church seems to them to be quite irrelevant . . . it is in this way, and in this way alone that the preacher, because he is also a pastor, can learn to translate his message so that it comes alive and gets across.

Not least important in supporting the contention

that the preacher who is also a faithful pastor will make a better preacher are the considerations which arise from the demand that every sermon should be preached with a burning sense of urgency to the heart of realised need. The needs of the individuals who compose the average congregation are quite incredibly varied, far more so than most ministers, immersed in the task of catering for those needs, have time to realise. A director of education, sitting at morning worship in the well-filled kirk which he faithfully attended, began to take stock of the situation, and went afterwards to his minister. 'Look', he said, 'I was sizing things up this morning and realised for the first time the following facts. You were expected this morning to deal with the needs of some 600 people. Between the children's address and the sermon to the adults you had to cover an age-group ranging from 3 years to 90 years; they were people of every temperament and outlook, and all levels of education and training, doing all sorts of jobs, coming from widely varied types of homes and backgrounds, living off every level of income, from old folk with nothing beyond the pension to comparatively wealthy men who could, if they wanted, have signed you a cheque for £1000 and hardly missed it. And if you could have taken the I.Q. of all that lot! It suddenly dawned upon me that we expect you ministers every Sunday to undertake an assignment we would never dream of thrusting on any teacher, however able and experienced'. That is only a dramatic statement of a situation which continually faces every preacher. How is he to keep in touch with all the changing needs of so wide a variety of people? If he confines his pastoral care to the visitation of the sick, the old, the bereaved, will the emphasis of his message not inevitably become one-sided? Great though the needs unquestionably are of his members in such situations, and prior claim though they must always have on the time and care of their pastor, for the greater part of the people to whom he has to preach, life is not made up always or mainly of sickness, age or sorrow; it is composed of the laughter and tears, the trials and temptations, the successes and failures that weave the web of daily living. That is why it seems a pity that so many assistants are given by their 'bishop' the visiting of only the sick and the old. They should be encouraged also to visit ordinary people in the normal life of home at all its ages and stages. They will learn more then, and in their later ministry, about human nature, its strength and weakness, in the homes of the people than in many a Psychology class; they will learn by practice, through trial and error, the difficult but indispensable art of handling people, as it can never be taught in pure theory by any expert in Pastoral Theology. It is in this field of sheer, hard routine work that a preacher is kept aware of all the varied needs of the whole of his flock, if he is being diligent here he will never require to be reminded that under the seemingly placid surface of their lives as they sit there in the pews run strong currents of desire and need, hope or fear. He will be on the exact wave-length of their need, and as he looks down on them from the pulpit he will know, deep down within himself: 'This that I have to say is true, and relevant, and vital for them'. Then he will preach with both ardour and accuracy.

Before departing from this topic of the preacher's complementary function as pastor, a word at least must be said about the character of pastoral visitation, and the best use of the opportunities it affords. The vexed question inevitably presents itself 'To pray, or not to pray?' Often the answer may be obvious and inescapable. With the sick and the old, and all the people classified by our American brethren as 'shut-ins', always pray, surely. They cannot come to Church, you are taking the Church to them; they may never hear you preach a sermon . . . here is your God-given chance to make local and personal the Gospel you proclaim to the many. With ordinary 'district' visiting the problem is more complex, and a middle course has to be steered between forcing prayer or family worship in a situation where the atmosphere is all wrong and missing a chance when it is offered. What is a minister to do when he finds himself of an evening in a home in a housing scheme, the children, pyjama-clad, grouped on the carpet round the TV set? Father, a little awk-wardly, goes and turns down the sound, leaving on the picture, while mother sweeps a chair clear of impedimenta. Attention wanders generally during the conversation with this unwonted (perhaps unwanted) visitor. The climax is reached when one of the children creeps forward and turns up the sound again. How is a man to pray, naturally and reverently, against the unfair competition of Wells Fargo or Dotto? On the other hand the pastor dare never forget that he is there as the representative of Christ and His Church, that in the nature of things he will not be in that home very often, and that he dare not fail to take any opportunity to make real in that home the continuing presence of Him Who neither comes nor goes, but is with His people all the days, remembering, and if need be reminding them, that these parents by their vows as Church members and the vows they took when their children were baptised have openly declared their willingness to make room and find time for Christ. For what it is worth as personal experience, one has often been sorry afterwards that one did not take or make a chance to pray, but never sorry when one did.

No study of the preacher's task in relation to the rest of his duties would be complete without some attempt to set the sermon in its context within the Service as a whole. How much time and care should a preacher give to planning the Service as a whole, and preparing the prayers and devotions, when he must perforce devote most of his time and energy to preparing his sermon? Here, again, it is essential to preserve a sense of proportion. There is a dreadful phrase, still used occasionally in Scotland, whereby the prayers, and praise and Scripture Lessons, indeed all that goes before the sermon in public worship, is referred to as the 'preliminary exercises'. This is only equalled by the practice so common in churches in the United States, where members of the congregation may come in any time during the first half-hour of the Service, at suitable stages designated by asterisks on the printed Order of Service, when anything up to 200 people may be shown to their seats by the ushers. To the startled visitor, bred in the old tradition of getting in before the bell stops, this tends to suggest that it is all right as long as you get in before the 'big feature' comes on! Perhaps we Scots have too long made too much of the sermon as the centre of the Service, the 'big feature' to which all else forms only the 'preliminary exercises'. However that may be, surely the whole Service needs careful preparation, and not only the sermon, if merely on the grounds that the sermon itself will meet with a more responsive hearing if the people have been 'tuned in' already by prayer and praise and the reading of the Word of God which the sermon is now to open to them. In this connection there are two theories which may be adopted. One is that the whole Service should strike the same note and develop the same theme as the sermon, the prayers, the praise, the Scripture Lessons will all move in the same direction, so that one cumulative effect is produced, and one clear impression left by the total worship. This will obviously happen, in any case, on the occasion of the great festivals of the Christian year, but many men adopt this as their deliberate policy, one which has much to be said for it. Its one danger is that by striking one particular note it may miss some other of the many needs represented in the congregation at any one Service. The note of one Service may be challenge, that note and none other may ring throughout it all, yet there must be at every Service some soul desperately needing, not challenge, but comfort, and that need must not be neglected. That is why the traditional elements of adoration, confession, supplication, thanksgiving, and intercession still constitute the *sine qua non* of adequate Christian worship, bringing all the varied needs of our many-sided human nature to the God

77

Who created and alone can recreate us, and preparing, in the only right and proper fashion for the proclaiming and receiving of His Word, the living, lasting Word of God.

If the total pattern of the Service be thus regarded and so prepared there are two somewhat controversial points which cannot be overlooked . . . the place, if any, of a Children's Address, and the length, desirable or ideal, of the sermon. Concerning the Children's Address it might be said, not inappropriately, that it resembles the famous little girl who had a little curl, that grew in the middle of her forehead . . . when it is good it is very, very good, and when it is bad it is horrid. It must not, and be it said, it need not, be an intrusion in the worship, and this impression of an intrusion can be avoided if the talk to the children deals with the same theme as the main sermon, or at least handles some cognate idea. It must be remembered that in very many congregations in the larger towns and cities, where the members come from a widely scattered area the one practicable expedient to enable children and parents to attend together even when the children are quite young is that commonly adopted, of having the children come to the beginning of Morning Service, and then go out to Sunday School, travelling home with their parents after the Service. What more fitting than that during that first period of the Service room should be made and opportunity taken for a short word specifically for the children, helping them to feel that they have a place of their own in their Father's House, and are not merely there on sufferance . . . an insufferable idea! This method has been proved to encourage the parents to attend, and many a grown-up has been heard to remark that he enjoys the Children's Address . . . he understands it!

Concerning the ideal length of sermon it would be presumptuous to lay down hard and fast rules. There is a growing school of thought which will go so far to meet the modern inability to concentrate as to insist that anything over fifteen minutes is too long. But how can any man deal adequately with any of the great themes of the Christian faith in about the operational time required for a haircut (masculini generis)? One recalls queueing up at 8 o'clock on a Sunday morning during student days in Zurich, to stand through the whole Service, while Emil Brunner preached on the Ten Commandments, never for less than forty-five minutes, any less and the people would have felt cheated. Much depends on the preacher, the subject and the particular situation.

Lest the final emphasis seem to be left on such questions of practical detail, which would surely be a mistake, let another familiar saying of Principal Martin have the last word. 'Gentlemen', he was wont to say, 'when you are in a charge of your own, and going about your pastoral duties, you will often find yourself outside a door, knocking, or ringing the bell, and wishing with all your heart that it might not open, because behind that door lies some situation of sin, suffering or sorrow with which you feel quite incompetent to deal. When you feel like that, always remind yourself that Christ is behind that door already, and at work. All you have to do is to make real His presence and power'. Whether you function as the pastor who also preaches on Sunday, or the preacher who dare never forget he is also a pastor, there is the fundamental and inspiring truth, Christ is at work already behind every door, and in every life. All you have to do is to make real His presence and power.

V

SPECIALISED TECHNIQUES FOR SPECIAL
OPPORTUNITIES CONFRONTING
THE PREACHER

No study of the peculiar tasks which face the
preacher in fulfilling his function in the contemporary situation would be complete without some
careful consideration being given to the fact that almost
any preacher may find himself called upon, sooner or
later, to preach in unusual circumstances which are
challenging enough to cause him great concern, if not
positive dismay. The vast bulk of his preaching may
still be done to his own normal congregation in a
Church, Sunday by Sunday, and our previous study
has been deliberately related, as is only right, to the
problems with which he must reckon there, regularly
and as part of the ordinary run of his work. He will
remember that the man in the pew is still modern man,
although he may still be influenced and affected,
though not necessarily consciously so, by all the subtle
atmosphere of a Church Service, by the general sense
of worship, and by a long-accepted tradition of reverent
listening to preaching which conforms to a certain
recognised and expected pattern. As we have repeatedly
emphasised, too much must no longer be taken for
granted even here, for gone are the days when a country
congregation would listen with avidity, every critical
faculty of the weaver, and the blacksmith as well as

the dominie on a hair-trigger of sensitivity to any hint of heresy; when at the instructed and often heated after-discussions round the fire in the 'smiddy', or leaning over the bridge watching the burn-water tumble down to the sea, this young man, fresh from College, was written off as poor thin stuff, for with the modern craze for brevity he had got no further than 'seventhly and finally, my brethren', while another was damned beyond redemption because, in spite of his fine periods and polished oratory, he was not 'sound on the fundamentals'.

To us all this sounds like a quaint echo out of another world, unbelievably remote, alike in time and space, which, of course, it is.

Illustrating further the total change in the situation, is the famous occasion from the latter years of Queen Victoria's reign. It was the time-honoured custom that one of the guest preachers invited to Crathie Kirk during Her Majesty's holiday months at Balmoral should be the Moderator of the General Assembly of the Church of Scotland for that year. A problem presented itself. One particular Moderator was an eminent ecclesiastic and a most able administrator (for which virtues he had, no doubt, been chosen) but he was notorious far and wide for his lengthy, ponderous, and incredibly dull sermons, a combination of gifts and defects which is not altogether unknown, even at a later date! According to protocol he must preach before the Queen, and any failure to invite him would be regarded as a grave omission, if not a direct insult. So, invited he was, but first a strong and influential deputation of leading Churchmen waited upon the

Right Reverend gentleman and pointed out that Her Majesty was in rather indifferent health and could not be expected to sit too long, that she was accustomed to brief snippets of addresses from her Anglican Chaplains, hardly worth calling 'sermons' at all, and that in all the circumstances it would be advisable on this occasion for the preacher to depart from his usual practice of giving his hearers a good solid meal of the strong meat of the Word, and preach a short sermon. The good man heard them out, and then replied that he fully realised the cogency of their contentions, and found the request eminently reasonable; that one must, of course, respect the wishes of Her Majesty; so that, while it went against the grain, and would mean most deliberate and careful effort, he would endeavour to keep his discourse within the hour!

These days are gone, even for normal preaching in Church. Now we have to reckon with a complete swing of the pendulum in the opposite direction and the preacher must be prepared, on occasion, to proclaim the Gospel in a situation totally unlike that which prevails in any Church, to an audience which bears no resemblance whatsoever to a worshipping, expectant congregation.

There are, for example, all the widely-varied and altogether challenging opportunities which have arisen in connection with modern efforts and experiments in evangelism. In Scotland since the Second World War, there have been the Christian Commando Campaigns, Visitation Evangelism Campaigns in a wide variety of areas and Religion and Life Campaigns of many types. All the different types of effort have been

F*   83

co-ordinated in the 'Tell Scotland' Movement, including concentrated and highly specialised efforts on the unprecedented scale of the Billy Graham All-Scotland Crusade, and the less spectacular but no less effective continued efforts made by groups of local Churches, or by each Church within its own parish, to reach and win the careless and the ignorant around their own doors. Running on parallel lines is the whole development of Industrial Chaplaincies, through which the Church seeks to establish, develop and strengthen her contact with the 'working-classes', to use that much overworked term, who are reputed to have no interest whatsoever in the worship, work and witness of the Church, all of which they regard as being entirely irrelevant to the real issues of life. In any or all of these types of effort any local minister may well find himself involved, either because he personally shares this interest in evangelism or because he cannot evade a sense of obligation towards those few among the Churchless many whom he cannot but regard as his personal responsibility simply because he is a minister of the Gospel. How is he to approach the task, which may well go completely against the grain, and from which he may shrink with every fibre of his being, the task of speaking in the most unsuitable situation to an audience unprepared, and, at least at first, un-welcoming, if not hostile?

Unsuitable and unlikely to a degree such situations may well be. Here are some from actual experience . . . a three-minute talk to a Saturday night crowd in a cinema, looking across the glare of footlights at a sea of faces that are only dim blurs of lesser shadow; a talk to a group at the same table in a works canteen, amid the clatter of a serve-yourself service with tin trays!; an address to a crowded meeting of a Glasgow Rangers F.C. Supporters' Club, very much there on sufferance; a two-minute address in a dance-hall, the speaker introduced with a roll of drums; one has been given for a pulpit a pile of sleepers in a railway repair shed, an upturned empty bottle crate on the sawdust-strewn floor of a public house bar, the top of a step-ladder outside a fair-ground, the back of a lorry, the bumper of a car. How is one to set about dealing with such a situation, where you start 'from scratch' with everything against you, where nothing can be taken for granted in previous knowledge, or interest in and sympathy with the object of your visit? This problem confronts every preacher who is ever called to speak in an unlikely situation, though it may not present quite such dramatic difficulties as some of those we have outlined.

The first concern of the preacher in these circumstances must be to steady himself by recalling his essential function and primary purpose, which are no different because the situation may be fantastically different. After all a doctor comes to heal, first and foremost, whether he exercises his healing function amid the sterilised equipment and smooth, organised efficiency of an operating theatre, or performs an emergency amputation under appalling conditions to release a man trapped by a fall of rock in a mine or caught by tumbled twisted steel in the wreckage of a train disaster. The preacher is there, in that cinema, works canteen, dance-hall, public house, fairground or whatever it may be to preach the Gospel of Jesus Christ, and proclaim His presence, power and Kingship, he is there to make a road and build a bridge for Christ to enter into some life that otherwise might never know Him, to speak to these particular people as a man speaketh with his friend some living, vital word, as from Christ, to teach and convince, to comfort or to challenge and to win their response. The strange and fascinating fact is that, in personal experience, exactly the same rules laid down for preaching under normal circumstances in a Church, hold good in these very different situations, and their validity has been proved again and again. Indeed they are more important than ever, and any departure from them or failure to give them their due priority is visited immediately and inevitably by complete disaster.

Every man attempting, or allowing himself to be drawn into such a special effort must realise at the outset that a special technique is necessary. It is quite hopeless to take last Sunday's sermon and whittle it down, or trim it to size; one has never known that method to work yet. It is much harder to give a three-minute talk on a Saturday evening in a cinema to an audience there for entertainment, than to deliver a thirty-minute sermon in Church on Sunday morning to a congregation gathered to worship. The three-minute talk may well need much more careful preparation! A different technique is obligatory, but the fundamental message and emphasis is the same. Out of a not inconsiderable experience in this special field of going where the people are, and speaking to them wherever they will listen, covering a wide variety of

effort and extending over a period of years these impressions stand out in retrospect with striking clearness
. . . It is the man who preaches Christ, sincerely,
directly, simply, with conviction and without apology,
who is listened to with respect, deepening to eagerness
and a strange hunger by men and women of all sorts,
in every kind of situation. The man who tells a crowd
of workers in a canteen or at a factory gate, quite
simply, what Christ had done for others, what Christ
has done for him, and can do for them is using an
argument and an appeal to which the Communist has
no answer. The speaker who goes straight to the heart
of things without winding about the matter with
circumstance, and speaks of the great fundamentals of
the faith, God and His ways with men, man and his
unsatisfied hunger for God, why we are here, where we
go from here, the mysteries of sin, suffering and death,
will receive from the average working-man and
working-woman a hearing and an interest accorded,
surprising as it may seem, to no political speaker, and
no concert party. The man, who, out of a personal
knowledge of Christ, and not from any mere technical
cleverness, answers the questions men put to him with
honesty and directness, speaking in the language they
understand to the heart of their deepest need, too
seldom realised, is making the most of his time and his
chance.

This very special type of preaching,—for preaching,
as we have tried to demonstrate, for all its strangeness,
it still is in essence . . . searches, tries and often shews up
those who venture the effort. It can reveal unsuspected
weaknesses in the 'expertise' of the successful 'popular'

preacher, and conversely it can uncover unrealised capabilities in men who would regard themselves as plodding, earnest, undistinguished practitioners in the art of preaching; they surprise themselves and everyone else. What is required is sincerity, first and foremost, that ring of truth in the inward parts which comes through so clearly in the unusual setting, and is missed immediately and infallibly in that setting, whereas its absence may be covered up in the helpful atmosphere of a Church Service. Next to sincerity is directness and simplicity; in three minutes a man must get straight to the point and stay there, which is no bad exercise for those of us sermonisers who like to spread ourselves over a leisurely thirty minutes. Not least important is the possession in a unique degree of the faculty of adaptability. Very often some element in the very strangeness of the situation can provide a man with a heaven-sent, divinely-inspired opportunity, if he can but see and seize it. Some examples may well prove more helpful and illuminating than any amount of abstract theory and ideal principles.

First, the art of adaptability, which can be learned by experience. In a Christian Commando Campaign held in Edinburgh just shortly after the War a team of speakers were invited to a large departmental store, and given fifteen minutes of the firm's time to speak to the entire staff, except for a 'skeleton crew' left in each department. The leader was a clergyman from England with a wide experience of this particular technique. He began by saying, 'No doubt you are wondering why we are here. Well, I have been on this kind of job many times. I have been sent into fire stations to kindle in the firemen a new fire of love and loyalty to Jesus Christ, I've been sent into bus depots to start the drivers and conductors on a new route that will take them where they really want to go; I was once sent into a famous gramophone factory to help one man here and another there to listen, for perhaps the first time to His Master's Voice; and we've come here today to open up a new department in the lives of some of you.' This was in the days when rationing was still in full force, and your ration book contained a page headed 'Personal Points' which were used for precious goods like sweets, etc. When this particular team reported back the Campaign Leader said to the 'new department' leader, rather challengingly, 'You're going this afternoon to address the staff in the Food Office. What will you talk about to them?' Like a flash came back the answer: 'Personal Points'! This kind of approach may, of course, be written off as a mere 'tour de force', a piece of sleight-of-hand carried out with words and ideas, albeit religious ideas, a somewhat superficial bit of applied cleverness, so here are two further examples, shewing how much deeper an audience can be carried in a few swift stages.

During that same Campaign in Edinburgh a minister was assigned to give a short talk in a cinema. He took the assignment very seriously, so much so that he visited the cinema the day before, and sat through the entire programme into which he sought to integrate, if he could, his brief message. His pains 'paid off'. The next evening the audience were edified by a gangster film, entitled: 'They made him a Fugitive' which told, in grim detail, the story of a young lad who got into trouble, fell in with a gang of crooks, became more and more deeply committed, to die in the end a miserable violent death in a running fight with the police. The last sequence faded out on a shot of the bullet-riddled body of the lad sprawled on the sidewalk. This picture faded, our minister walked forward to the footlights and began like this, '*They* made him a fugitive? *They* made him a fugitive? Every one of us in this cinema knows perfectly well that he made himself a fugitive, when he started running away from ordinary hard work, running away from his first mistake because he would not face up to it. That's what's wrong with all of us, we are all somewhere fugitives from God.' From that moment he led them deep into the realities of sin and grace. Three years later, in a similar situation in a large Glasgow cinema an Englishman, an evangelical Anglo-catholic, began to capture the interest of the Saturday evening entertainment-seeking crowd, by saying that he had been most interested to watch with them, a few moments previously, the 'trailer' of the film 'Odette', the story of Odette Churchill who was captured by the Germans when helping to organise the French Resistance movement and cruelly tortured. He told how he had visited the film studios while part of the film was being shot, and had talked with Miss Anna Neagle who played the name part. 'She told me', he said, 'that it was a very difficult part to play.' She had to convey a sense of the horror Odette suffered, and yet make her heroism supreme, make real the cruelty, and yet let the sacrifice of it all stand out. 'I shall never forget,' he added very quietly, 'how simply she stated that she had been helped more than anything by remembering all the time Another Who was dropped into enemy-occupied territory 2000 years ago, and didn't get away with His life.' From that moment he had that whole vast crowd of people at the foot of the Cross, and for the rest of his three minutes he kept them there.

Someone may well ask, 'Do the results of such special efforts, demanding the development of their own techniques and making demands as they must on the skill and sincerity of the men taking part, ever make the effort worth while?' Whatever the results, measured in terms of additions to Church membership or any other recognised method of 'Counting scalps', from the point of view of any preacher who thus ventures out of the comparative shelter and security of his pulpit and his Church such effort is infinitely rewarding. Any justification one might require for including so full a study of this subject in the Warrack Lectures is the number of working ministers, of all denominations, and every age-group and type who have borne witness to the fact that in the effort they have made to do something so challengingly different they have rediscovered the relevance and power of the Gospel they preached in the routine ministry Sunday after Sunday. They have added both to the ardour and the accuracy of their preaching.

There are two more highly specialised tasks for the preacher, each raising its own peculiar problems and offering its quite unusual challenge, which certainly merit some careful consideration. No survey of the field of possible opportunities in the present situation would be adequate without some reference to broadcasting and television. As far as can be ascertained no specific study of the problems and techniques involved in these two highly-influential spheres for proclaiming the Gospel has so far been included in any series of Warrack Lectures, but such a study is surely within the terms of reference of the original deed, although the unique influence of these two media, for better, for worse, could never have been foreseen when this Lectureship was founded. One makes no apology for incorporating such a study in this series, and that for two good reasons. Here in Scotland the British Broadcasting Corporation, under the direction of the Rev. Dr. Ronald Falconer, Director of Religious Broadcasting, are making it their deliberate policy to cast their net wide, and to allow the voices of younger men to be heard on the radio, indeed they are anxious to learn of 'up and coming' new voices in the pulpits of Scotland. It is not fanciful therefore to assume that any of the regular students for whom these Lectures are primarily intended may have it as his dream or his dread, that he might be called upon to address this strange, unseen audience, either by conducting Children's Hour Prayers, or by leading the ordinary Morning or Evening Broadcast Service, and he would be none the worse of having some idea how to face this unusual assignment. It has also to be remembered that many of those who are reached by these Lectures, as originally delivered, or as they may be published later, will be carrying out their ministry in the United States, where even a town of 50,000 inhabitants may have two radio stations, where it is not unknown for a particular congregation to operate its own radio station, and where, therefore, such opportunities may come the way of the average minister much more often. How shall a preacher address himself to this quite different task?

He must first choose what his emphasis shall be. He may decide that he will simply conduct an ordinary Service, thinking, as usual, of the congregation immediately and visibly before him, and rest content that the unseen congregation should be graciously permitted to eavesdrop, as it were, at an act of worship which has no special relation to them. But this, surely, is to deny or ignore practically every principle so far laid down in these Lectures. What a chance a man has here to proclaim the Gospel of Christ to some in that unseen audience (one can hardly call it a congregation) who otherwise have never heard, what a God-given challenge to open up a road and build a bridge for Christ to enter into some life into which He has often tried to enter, but in vain; above all, what a unique setting for speaking personally as one man to another and not at all as a preacher haranguing a multitude, a word in season, as from the Lord. Surely the emphasis ought to be on the unseen listeners, and the congregation should be made to see that they are sharing in sending out from the Church where they worship regularly, a message, to which their praises and prayers, the whole atmosphere they help to create, can contribute in a subtle but real way. They should be encouraged to visualise (and the minister should be the first to do this himself) the kind of people to whom the Service will go, and the sort of circumstances in which they will listen. These are many and varied, and before the preacher even begins to prepare he should let his imagination picture those hearers and their situations, with understanding and sympathy.

First and most obvious are the various categories of 'shut-ins', the folk who are familiar with a Church Service and miss it badly, those too old or infirm to travel, the sick and those who are busy tending them at home, mothers baby-sitting with their own young children, people involved in necessary and inevitable Sunday duties. It is not always realised how much a radio Service is appreciated by listeners such as these. In the very early days of broadcast Services an old Scotswoman gave her minister her own impressions of listening in to one for the first time. 'Eh!' she said, 'it was maist wonderful. I could even hear the folk coughing and the umbrellas going dunt in the stands at the end of the pews! It was wonderful . . . but it wasn't the same as being there.' People like that must never be forgotten, and their needs must be ever before the preacher. Then there are the very many who have had some connection with the Church, but for one reason or another never go now; they still listen to broadcast Services, indeed, what one might call 'radio-religion' has become their undemanding, bargain-price Christianity. The preacher has their ear; can he speak some word to win them back to their forgotten allegiance? By no means least important are the very large number who have no Church-background, and no Church-connection but are there, tuned-in, and could be made to listen. It is surprising the number of homes in which the radio is turned on for the news in the morning and just left on, almost like a fine spray, falling softly on the ear, making no impact on the consciousness, until something makes what is coming out of this box of gadgets come alive and come home to someone who then starts to listen. What can the preacher do to see that this happens?

It is strange how very important it is for the preacher to direct his message, under these circumstances. Here is the greatest of all gaps needing to be bridged between the preacher and his hearers. Between him and them is interposed this highly artificial medium, this 'devilish invention' called a microphone, which not only stands between him and them, but picks up and reveals and conveys not only every peculiarity of accent, tone and expression but also with cruel and implacable accuracy an impression of sincerity or insincerity, carrying, even more than the direct spoken word, the ring of conviction, or the hollow, echoing lack of it. In order to bridge this gap, of mechanical medium, sundering miles, of course, mutual invisibility, the preacher's own colour of thought and imagination, as he speaks, are supremely important, if he is to 'get across'. The most deadly experience of this nature is to conduct for a whole week the series of 'Lift Up Your Hearts' talks at 7.50 in the morning. You go into a studio, sit at a table with the 'mike' confronting you, wait, with your tongue cleaving to the roof of your mouth, till the green light goes on, speak for four-and-a-half minutes, and then stagger home for breakfast, having seen two cleaners and one sleepy engineer. You have spoken, in the name of God, to several millions of people, who could never be gathered together in one place, in any sports arena in Great Britain or even in the famous Hollywood Bowl. It is quite futile to picture a vast audience gathered like that. You must think of and speak to the condition of the housewife bustling between kitchenette and breakfast table, frying-pan in hand, breadwinners snatching a hurried last mouthful as they run for bus or train, school-children being got off to school, with much mutual irritation. The same principle holds good of broad-casting a Church Service. Picture a patient in hospital, propped up in bed with earphones on, or the walking patients grouped round a set at the end of the ward; picture a shepherd and his family in their cottage high up among the hills, ten long walking miles or more from the nearest Church; the one solitary remaining inhabitant of a small island in the Orkneys; the cook in his galley on a fishery-protection cruiser, bucking through a rough sea in the Western approaches; the driver of a car making his way South through the Border Hills who has just switched on his car radio; a tired working-man having his Sunday long lie, in bed with his Sunday papers, but with the set still switched on. Picture these, and speak to these.

As far as preparation is concerned some special considerations must be noted. The British Broadcasting Corporation timing is meticulous to the split second, and it has to be. So must the preacher's timing be, and that for every part of the whole Service. Here is a splendid chance to 'ginger up' an organist who revels in rallentandoes! On one broadcasting occasion a certain congregation took 35 seconds to sing the first verse of a six-verse Hymn and 50 to sing the last! Nothing will so quickly kill such a Service for the

96

listener. For the sake of timing the sermon will almost certainly have to be written, word for word, which may be a real handicap to those of us who are accustomed to a freer method, and care must be taken to overcome the danger that the delivery becomes stilted. Somehow the preacher must convey to the unseen listener the impression: 'This man is not haranguing a congregation. This man is speaking to me, as man to man.' To achieve this end, avoid like the plague pious platitudes, religious cliches and parsonical inflections of the voice; speak if you can with a picture in your mind of actual people who you know will be listening, and speak to their condition; proclaim with directness, simplicity and sincerity the Gospel of Jesus Christ, and it is the unanimous witness of all preachers who have ever used this challenging medium that God will use you in ways past your finding out, humbling, uplifting and inspiring.

Lastly, in a word, what of Television, that latest medium whose possibilities for the persuasive proclamation of the Gospel, we have hardly begun to realise? It is interesting and significant that a group of our own divinity students should have recently been invited by the British Broadcasting Corporation to visit the studios, and try themselves out in various ways for television. Let it be recognised at once that to conduct a Service on TV, especially in the atmosphere of a studio is infinitely more searching than taking any kind of Service on what is known by the strange name of 'steam radio'. To sit there in the glare and heat of the lights, with the penumbra of technicians, like so many weird acolytes at some fantastic witches' sabbath, to talk into anything so deadly impersonal and yet so revealingly personal as the lens of a TV camera, feeling that your very soul is left naked as a new-born babe, that may make even the most experienced preacher lose his nerve and self-possession and with them the thread of what he planned to say. Some men are so utterly unnerved by it that they just cannot use this medium; some conversely come into their own; whereas they were handicapped by their voices when they could only be heard, now that they can be seen also they get across supremely well, they really communicate. Of course, there are all sorts of advantages, for the preacher can use, and that most effectively, many kinds of 'Visuals', finding an entrance for his message by 'Eye-gate' as well as 'Ear-gate' as Bunyan would have put it. One law must simply be recognised and accepted. The speaker, whatever he is talking about, must look and speak straight to the camera. If he is looking down at notes, however surreptitiously, half his effectiveness is lost. There is an aid known as a teleprompter, which shews on a screen, attached to the side of the camera the words that the speaker is supposed to be saying; but the moment he looks with that deviation of only a hair's breadth away from the lens of the camera the viewer loses the feeling: 'This man is speaking to me'. Thus strangely does this most modern invention drive home the root essential meaning of a 'sermon', whatever form it may take. The preacher must convey the impression that he is speaking, not merely to the many, but home to the individual heart of personal need; he must communicate himself, his unmistakable sincerity, his ardour of conviction and enthusiasm for the Gospel he proclaims,. and that Gospel must be directed with unerring accuracy, without wavering, as one man might look straight into the eyes of another.

We have come a long way, from our laying down of principles, theories, ideals for those who would preach to modern man in the present situation. No doubt we have advocated too many counsels of perfection. Let the emphasis rest, now, at the end, on a word of encouragement for all of us who preach, for none of us can ever distantly approach even the ideals we set ourselves. 'No one' cried a Scots preacher, 'no one ever has any right to despise a sincere and honest attempt to express something essential to the life of man'. What we as preachers have to express is more essential than ever to the life of real men and women. Let us express it with sincerity and honesty, with ardour and accuracy. Then no one will ever have any right to despise it, and most certainly God will not.